W9-BLG-320

CONTENTS

For Larry, Mark,
Mom, and Dad

Dan O'Keefe

The
Real
FESTIVUS

The True Story Behind

America's Favorite

Made-up Holiday

A PERIGEE BOOK

The Berkley Publishing Group
Published by the Penguin Group
Penguin Group (USA) Inc.
375 Hudson Street, New York, New York 10014, USA
Penguin Group (Canada), 90 Eglinton Avenue East, Suite 700, Toronto, Ontario M4P 2Y3, Canada (a division of Pearson Penguin Canada Inc.)
Penguin Books Ltd., 80 Strand, London WC2R 0RL, England
Penguin Group Ireland, 25 St. Stephen's Green, Dublin 2, Ireland (a division of Penguin Books Ltd.)
Penguin Group (Australia), 250 Camberwell Road, Camberwell, Victoria 3124, Australia (a division of Pearson Australia Group Pty. Ltd.)
Penguin Books India Pvt. Ltd., 11 Community Centre, Panchsheel Park, New Delhi—110 017, India
Penguin Group (NZ) cnr. Airborne and Rosedale Roads, Albany, Auckland 1310, New Zealand (a division of Pearson New Zealand Ltd.)
Penguin Books (South Africa) (Pty.) Ltd., 24 Sturdee Avenue, Rosebank, Johannesburg 2196, South Africa

Penguin Books Ltd., Registered Offices: 80 Strand, London WC2R 0RL, England

Copyright © 2005 by Dan O'Keefe
Text design by Pauline Neuwirth
Cover art and design by Ben Gibson

Printing History
Perigree trade paperback edition / November 2005

ISBN: 0-399-53229-3

PERIGEE is a registered trademark of Penguin Group (USA) Inc.
The "P" design is a trademark of Penguin Group (USA) Inc.

This book has been cataloged by the Library of Congress

PRINTED IN THE UNITED STATES OF AMERICA

10 9 8 7 6 5 4 3 2 1

FESTIVUS

THE BANE OF MY EXISTENCE

By Jason Alexander

Clearly, *Seinfeld* **was** one of those shows that do more than entertain—it becomes a source of pop culture. The chronicle of phrases and fads that were generated by our nine-season run is seemingly endless: "hand," mimbo, mansierre, puffy shirt, man hands, low talker, master of the domain, "yada-yada," Pez, Frogger, "Serenity Now," Vandalay Industries, the "move," marble rye, antidentite, Junior Mint. Trust me—it's endless.

Because of the show's enduring popularity, my daily life is a series of quotes and questions from legions of diehard fans. I am genuinely pleased with the knowledge that our efforts continue to entertain so many. And I am constantly fascinated with how much in-depth knowledge the fans have of our program. But there is a downside, as well.

I cannot walk down the street without shouts of "George" or "Can't Stand Ya" following me. I have been asked more times than Steinbrenner what I think is going on inside the Yankee organization. The novelty of people yelling, "Where's Jerry?" or "Say hey to Kramer" has long ago worn off. I am constantly asked why I killed Susan; who won the contest; and whose bitch I became in prison.

All this I bear with dignity and humility because of my love of the show and my appreciation of our fans.

However, one question alone rises beyond all others. One question gets tossed at me from all directions until I am so psychically battered that I must limp to some retreat, away from all humanity, until I can summon the strength to once again face my Seinfeldian destiny. The question?—"What are you doing for Festivus?"

Festivus! FESTIVUS!!!!!

For one miserable episode, the Costanza family invited the world to join them for an inane, bizarre anti-holiday called Festivus. It wasn't a major story point. It wasn't a recurring story line. It was one lousy episode. It was brought to our table by a young writer named Dan O'Keefe. The truth was that this odd fellow had spent years celebrating (if that's the appropriate word) this freakish creation of his own father's slightly off-kilter mind. He proposed it as a notion for something the character of Frank Costanza, George's father, might have manufactured. It was to be a minor element, a throwaway—nothing.

But, since we were the show about nothing—the damn thing took! Upon airing the episode, Festivus parties popped up everywhere. Festivus ceremonies were proposed. The Ben and Jerry Ice Cream company created a Festivus flavor. Last rumor I heard was that the federal government was considering making it a national holiday.

And then the questions—the endless, mindless questions: How do we celebrate? What is the history? When is the exact date? Is there religious significance? One dumbass inquiry after another.

For years, all I could say when bombarded with this lunacy was, "For God's sake people, it's a TV show! Get a grip. Move on." But the glaring disappointment on their faces was too hard to take. It was like telling a little Christian child that there is no Santa. I had no stomach for it. Maybe because I'm Jewish. Maybe I'm just soft.

But now, like a ray of light direct from Heaven, my prayers have been answered, my personal salvation has arrived. You hold in your hands the definitive tome on Festivus. And it comes from the highest authority—Dan O'Keefe himself. Every question you have about this festival is answered in these pages. No effort has been spared. Upon completion, you will be able to preserve the rich history and colorful pageantry of this most holy day yourself. For the true *Seinfeld* fan, this is required reading. For the casual passerby, it is a curious primer on how to create your own ritual for the ages.

I realize that this book is also a shameless attempt to cash in on an international phenomenon. It is airport or bathroom reading at its best. I don't care. I'm free, dammit! At last, this burden has been lifted from me. From this day forward I can field these absurd missives by simply pointing to this ignoble publication. I recommend it with sincerity and passion. It is also pretty damn funny.

So enjoy. It is a Festivus gift from the Costanzas and the O'Keefes. God bless us, every one. And Happy Festivus, a festival for the rest of us.

—Jason Alexander, June 2005

FESTIVUS

WHAT'S UP WITH THAT?

So you think the holiday known as Festivus involves a metal pole, do you? Feats of strength? Commercial breaks? WRONG. That's just the television version. Because a network audience couldn't possibly have handled the real thing. A family huddled around a table by candlelight one random evening a year, eating and drinking too much, singing in German about a black pig, bitching about people who didn't like them into a barely functional tape recorder, and displaying obscene, hand-scrawled signs of a political nature.

But if you go beyond simple belief, if you are one of those lost souls who, captivated by the television portrayal of Festivus, actually celebrates the damn thing . . . what's up with that? Don't get out of the house much, do you? Maybe you should get a pet or a hobby or something. If you don't already have forty cats in your studio apartment, which will eat your eyes when you die, alone.

But as you may or may not know, this holiday actually existed even before it appeared on television. Our father invented it— our actual dad, Daniel O'Keefe Sr., not our Heavenly Father—our family celebrated it, and then one of us brothers stuck it on TV and bought a nice car with the money. The others received nothing, and were not allowed to touch or ride in the car. Yes, while Festivus is now apparently celebrated here and there around the country according to the principles set forth in the sitcom version, the reality of this day was far more bizarre and sinister. Less like something from a comedy about zany, lovable New Yorkers, and more like something from the *X-Files*. Like if one of the "Lone Gunmen" had children, and they all lived under a power line.

In this book you will learn, should you choose, how to celebrate Festivus according to the true and ancient traditions that have guided it since its birth back in the mists of the 1960s. But be warned: the secrets of this book can be dangerous. Do not read it while driving a car; that would be a bad idea. Do not use it to hold down important papers on a desk; it is flimsy and your papers may blow away. If you handle it carelessly, you may sustain paper cuts that are not only painful, but may attract sharks while swimming at the beach. Also, the way things are going in this country, reading books might soon lead to your arrest and a one-way black helicopter ride to some kind of orbital prison, or forced labor on an undersea kelp farm. Depending on the judge you get.

THE NEED
FOR FESTIVUS

The celebration we call Festivus, because that is its name, was born in 1966, when our dad decided that he wanted a new holiday. Apparently, the ones we already had just weren't doing it for him. And to be fair, let's all admit there are some problems with the existing holidays:

HOLIDAY: PROBLEM

Holiday: Christmas

> **Problem:** Too commercialized. Let's be honest, it's not really news to anyone that Christmas has become less a celebration of Jesus' birthday, and more of a nation-wide ugly-sweater competition. And an excuse to waste millions of kilowatts lighting up rooftops, so that from space, whole neighborhoods must look like landing strips on the rooftops of whorehouses. Happy Birthday, Jesus.

Holiday: Halloween

> **Problem:** Halloween is pretty much just devil worship cloaked in a celebration of childhood diabetes and

vandalism. The only good thing about it is it single-handedly props up the candy, egg, shaving cream, toilet paper, and new-mailbox industries.

Holiday: Arbor Day
Problem: A holiday devoted to trees. What an exciting idea. You might want to stop reading for a few minutes if your pulse is racing. Look, even if Arbor Day started as some kind of cool, sinister, druidic, tree religion, it's lost its mojo now. In elementary school we planted trees on the school grounds each Arbor Day, and in second grade I had just won some spelling bee, so I had to read a description of the tree species while they planted the damn thing. Later, third graders pulled all the leaves off it and stuffed them in my mouth, ears, nose, and pants. So I hate Arbor Day, as well as the Eastern White Pine.

Holiday: Presidents' Day
Problem: A bastardized hybrid of Washington's and Lincoln's birthdays. Combined holidays are inherently stupid: would you celebrate Thanksoween? How about Christmassover? Hallowgiving? Individually Washington and Lincoln were great Americans; mushed together they're an excuse for mattress sales and TV ads where Pontiac dealers chop down papier-mâché cherry trees.

Holiday: Thanksgiving
Problem: Okay, this one's not bad. Except of course the way it calls to mind the genocide and forced relocation of millions of Native Americans. And the football games

on Thanksgiving are always such one-sided blowouts; it's all over in the first quarter.

Holiday: Columbus Day
   Problem: An Italian kid stole some baseball cards from me in fourth grade. 'Nuff said.

In any case, the way we first heard it, our dad decided he wanted a day of celebration that wasn't commercialized, some dead guy's birthday, or a bunch of pagan plant crap.

FESTIVUS
WHAT'S IN A NAME?

Nowadays Dad claims he "pulled the name out of the air." However, on other occasions, he has said it means "party" in Latin. Yet we could not seem to find it in any Latin dictionary. In fact, we couldn't find it in *any* dictionary. As Merriam-Webster Online said,

"The word you've entered isn't in the dictionary. But we have some suggestions for Festivus. Do you mean:

fastidious
festive
festivities
fascists
phagocytes
factitious
fascisti
face-lifts
face-to-face
phagocytose

Well, it certainly wasn't fastidious, it was festive when it wasn't alarming, it took a strong stand against fascism

(See: the FUCK FACISM sign), face-lifts were rarely performed, and I don't know what a phagocyte is, unless it's some kind of offensive slang for a Broadway musical. So that wasn't much help with where the word came from.

However, the word *festivus* does seem to be part of the scientific names of a lot of weird bugs and fish. For instance, *Asianellus festivus*, which was discovered by a C. L. Koch in 1834 appears to be some kind of horrible insect. There's a Southeast Asian bumblebee called *Bombus festivus* or *Festivobombus*. We also found an ugly South American fish called *Mesonauta festivus*. It is described as a "peaceful and graceful cichlid that deserves greater consideration . . ." and a "timid fish that should be kept in a fairly tall aquarium." Finally, we discovered a huge, hideous beetle called *Glaphyrus festivus*.

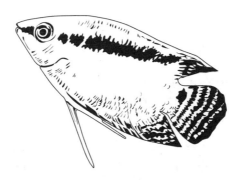

None of this has any bearing on the holiday Festivus, except insofar that it is a well-known fact that the Irish are related to bugs and fish. I believe the proportion is: 50 percent human, 20 percent goat, 20 percent bug, and 10 percent fish. Since our mother's mostly of English descent, that means we are only 10 percent bug and 5 percent fish.

THE SIGNIFICANCE AND ORIGIN OF FESTIVUS

You're probably wondering by this point, *What did your father originally intend to celebrate or commemorate when he made up this day, beyond just coming up with a new holiday that didn't suck as much as some of the others?* Well, my brothers and I wondered the same thing.

For a long time we just didn't know. Our folks literally wouldn't tell us. We had some theories, though:

THE HOLDOVER FROM THE COLLEGE FRATERNITY THEORY

BECAUSE ALL THREE of us brothers belonged to the same college organization, which had a lot of incredibly complicated yet pointless rituals, we naturally assumed Festivus might be related in some way to the rituals of my father's fraternity: the Columbia chapter of Phi Kappa Psi. We investigated:

DANNY: Dad, was any part of Festivus related to the rush or initiation rituals of your college frat?

DAD: No.

DANNY: Well, what were those rituals? I'll be the judge of whether they're Festivus-related.

DAD: There weren't any rituals. The fraternity was very happy to have new pledges. Oh, there was a secret handshake.

DANNY: What was it?

DAD: I think it was pretty much exactly the same as the Boy Scout handshake. I remember being somewhat disappointed.

DANNY: Yeah, that's not much of a ritual. Well, what did you do after initiation?

DAD: We went out and got drunk. Again.

DANNY: Again?

DAD: Again.

THE "EXPERIMENTING ON YOUR KIDS" THEORY

MEANING, WE WONDERED if our parents were just curious to see what would happen to their children if they had us celebrate some weird fake holiday. This may seem odd, that we suspected our folks of experimenting on us. Except that it happened before.

When I was a few months old, Dad read somewhere that if a baby carries the gene for schizophrenia, it will lack the "grab" reflex that all infant primates possess; that is, when it feels it is falling, its little arms will involuntarily clutch at the air, trying to catch hold of a branch in the trees where our ape ancestors once lived. Unless the infant is or will be schizophrenic, in which case it will not "grab." In any case, Mom came home and found Dad holding the month-old Danny by his feet, dangling him upside down in the air, to see if he would grab properly. When she yelled at him to stop, he shouted, "I'm trying to find out if he's schizophrenic!" Because this experiment was interrupted, the jury is still out on the schizo thing.

So one theory was that Mom and Dad were secretly documenting the effects of Festivus on us, and that they eventually intended to publish an article in some scientific journal, exposing the link between fake holidays and bed-wetting or serial arson. However, every experiment must involve a "control" group that doesn't get the pill or electric shock or bizarre celebration. And as far as we know, they didn't stash any other siblings of ours in a cave somewhere, who DIDN'T grow up celebrating it. And furthermore, that would be a crappy control group, because how the cave-kids turned out might have more to do with being raised in a cave than with not celebrating a fake holiday.

THE CLINICAL INSANITY THEORY

DOESN'T HOLD WATER. I mean, both parents are upstanding citizens who held down jobs, raised kids, and were never arrested (that we know of). They both hold advanced degrees. Mom taught college for years at Vassar and elsewhere, and has published two books of literary criticism:

Readers in Wonderland: The Liberating Worlds of Fantasy Fiction and *Good Girl Messages: How Young Women Were Misled by Their Favorite Books.* Our father wrote a six-hundred-page book: a unified field theory of sociology, anthropology, and psychology called *Stolen Lightning: The Social Theory of Magic* that was nominated for a National Book Award, but lost to a mediocre biography of Lyndon Baines Johnson. There's your clinical insanity right there. Revenge will be sweet when this volume wins a National Book Award, as it no doubt will.

THE TRUTH: THE FIRST DATE ANNIVERSARY

IN FACT, MY parents have finally admitted the first version of the holiday began as a celebration of their first date. On Lincoln's birthday 1962, my parents met for drinks at New York's Plaza Hotel, and then had dinner at a French restaurant called Le Veau d'or, then saw Gluck's opera *Orfeo ed Eurydice* at the Metropolitan Opera, then had drinks somewhere. That's a hell of a first date. Most of mine have usually involved a movie about a rogue cop who makes his own brand of justice.

In any case, our folks got married in 1963, and starting pretty much the next year, on the anniversary of their first date, they'd break out a bottle of champagne and look at the wedding photographs. In 1966 this solidified into a formal holiday. The name "Festivus" may have first been used in these early celebrations. However, I was born in 1968 and Larry in 1969, and under the pressure of child-rearing, the holiday kind of died out. But starting in about 1972 my father was fooling around with his Dictaphone (a primitive 1970s tape recorder that has inspired many puns over the years) given to him by Reader's Digest to tape interviews with freelance writers in his job as an editor there. He started taping the three of us: me (Danny), four; Larry, three; and Mark, about one. This reminded him of the Samuel Beckett play *Krapp's Last Tape*, which he had lent my mother on their first date, and which mostly consists of a man making audio-tapes and listening to ones he's already made.

This in turn reminded him of that first-date anniversary called Festivus he and my mom had once celebrated, and so he re-created and expanded this holiday, now including his children. This revived Festivus was first celebrated in 1975. There was a big dinner that was originally turkey, the only turkey we had every year besides Christmas and Thanksgiving; we mostly ate hot dogs and canned soup the rest of the time. The adults got champagne, and then we went upstairs to the living room, where we all looked at family pictures, and then Dad taped us all talking into the tape recorder about the past year.

Over the years it evolved, and bells and whistles were added—sometimes literally—but that's how it came together at first. It began in 1966, died out in 1969, was

A NOTE CONCERNING SAMUEL BECKETT'S KRAPP'S LAST TAPE

WHICH inspired the main component of the holiday, that is, the tape recordings. This play is about an ancient, bitter man, listening to tapes of himself as a middle-aged, depressed man, who is in turn listening to tapes of himself as a young, optimistic man.

So the centerpiece of Festivus is modeled upon one of the most depressing pieces of theater of the twentieth century. It is a tribute to our father's genius, man's indomitable spirit, American know-how, and the power of Pabst Blue Ribbon cold-brewed beer that this was turned into something that was only occasionally depressing or bitter. In fact, usually it was quite festive.

restarted in 1975, and the last tape recording was made in 1991, when the three of us kids were beginning the process of moving out to California. Mom and Dad both claim they no longer celebrate it. However, we are virtually certain that now we three brothers are out of the house, our parents have returned to the original celebration, just the two of them, a turkey, a bottle of something bubbly, and some photographs.

COMMON MISCONCEPTIONS ABOUT FESTIVUS

Though only a family of five originally celebrated Festivus, these days it is celebrated by literally dozens of prisoners, college students, and bored people in rural areas across this great nation. And some crappier nations like Canada and Uruguay. And God bless them all and keep them from rape and thresher accidents. But they're doing it *all wrong*.

If you want to celebrate Festivus the way we did, you should know the following things were *not* part of the original celebration:

THE POLE

THERE WAS NO pole in our holiday. That was a joke that we came up with for the show. I should mention at this point that the "Festivus" episode of *Seinfeld* (which was actually called "The Strike") was co-written with Jeff Schaffer and Alec Berg, and Mr. Seinfeld approved it, so much of the credit for bringing this holiday to the world, or blame for inflicting it on it, belongs to them.

So, no pole. We did have in the house this weird, old, antique pole-like thing, though: a long wooden stick with a blunt knob at the end, given to us by an antique dealer friend of Mom's. It was used to gently poke people who fell asleep in church, back in the 1700s in New England. But we never decorated it, except when my brothers and I put jelly on it and tried to stick it in each other's hair.

FATHER-SON WRESTLING

OH, COME ON. What are you, an idiot? Sure, we're Irish, but do you really think our dad forced us to wrestle him at the dinner table? If this had actually occurred, all three of us would have been taken away by Child Protective Services and raised by the State of New York while our dad went to jail and was forced to join a white supremacist gang for protection, while an episode of *Special Victims Unit* would have been written about us. No, the only time we wrestled with our dad on Festivus was when we didn't feel like celebrating the damn thing, and he had to chase us around the house and drag us back inside, which he also had to do when we had strep throat and didn't want to drink that disgusting syrupy antibiotic they had in the seventies.

Anyway, the three of us boys did frequently wrestle with each other on Festivus, but it was just standard-issue child-on-child warfare, over such things as who tore the head off my nude Lieutenant Uhura *Star Trek* action figure. (Answer: Larry, and he has since then been linked to twenty-six Uhura mutilations in eleven states, but not enough evidence exists to indict him.)

THE DATE: DECEMBER 23RD

OUR FESTIVUS HAD no set date. It was what you'd call a "floating holiday." It could occur at any time roughly between September and May. Although it happened with greater frequency in October and November, and between February and April. One year there were two, I believe. On several occasions, though, it coincided with Thanksgiving. Once it occurred on August sixth, although this was not in any way designed to commemorate the bombing of Hiroshima.

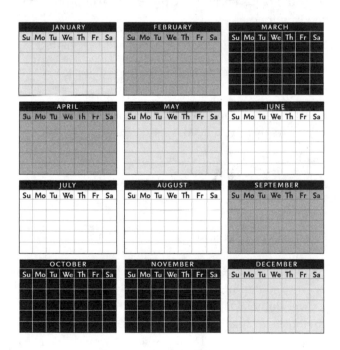

White: Risk of Festivus Low to None
Light Grey: Moderate Risk of Festivus
Dark Grey: High Risk of Festivus
Black: DANGER: FESTIVUS

The reasons for this "floating" nature of the holiday are unclear:

LARRY: Dad, why did Festivus have no set date?

DAD: I think it made it more exciting.

LARRY: So is that why?

MOM: No, it's because we never got around to choosing one.

DAD: We were very busy. It was hard to schedule.

MOM: We were raising three children, for goodness sake.

DAD: It's not enough your family has a special holiday all its own; you need a set date, too?

LARRY: I guess it would be nice.

DAD: (ominously) A lot of things would be nice.

LARRY: What does that mean?

DAD: Never you mind.

So we never knew exactly when it was coming, but there were sometimes hints that Festivus might be on the way. Over dinner Dad might whisper to Mom, "It's starting to look a lot like Festivus . . ." Or sometimes the moon would turn to blood, and four horsemen would ride across the sky and kill a third of the creatures that live in the sea. But most often, we'd just come home from school, and the house would be illuminated only by candlelight, and there'd be weird stuff hanging on the walls.

FESTIVUS SYMBOLS AND DECORATIONS

There may not have been a pole, but Festivus certainly did have its share of unique symbols, props, and just plain odd crap. Such as:

THE CLOCK AND THE BAG

THE CENTRAL SYMBOL of this holiday was not a pole. It was a clock and a bag. Sometimes a clock *in* a bag. But not always.

The significance of this remains unknown to this day. Mom and Dad simply won't discuss it. And never have.

1975:

DANNY: Daddy, what does the clock and the bag mean?

DAD: *(angrily)* That's not for you to know!

2005:

DANNY: Hey, Mom, what was the significance of the clock and the bag, anyway?

MOM: *(evasively)* Oh, who remembers?

It's possible that at the tail end of their first date, they shoplifted a clock from Macy's, hid it in a bag as they snuck out, and this furtive, illegal thrill became part of the holiday. Or that while walking home, they were jumped by a mugger, the old-fashioned kind in a black mask and striped shirt, and my father hit him in the head with the only weapon he had: a clock he had purchased earlier that day, still in its bag, which knocked the guy cold as Mom shrieked "My hero!" Actually, I don't know why that's the symbol,

A NOTE REGARDING THE VEAU D'OR RESTAURANT

WHERE this all started, with our folks' first date. The Veau d'Or is still there. It continues to serve delicious classical French cuisine at reasonable prices, in an elegant yet relaxed environment. It is located at 129 East 60th Street, across from Bloomingdale's, and serves dinner every night except Sunday. Try the veal.

it doesn't matter why, and I don't even want to know why. It just is.

THE ODD HEADGEAR

BEFORE THE FESTIVUS dinner that kicked off the Festivus-ivities, we were expected to change into relatively nice clothes. There was no ritual costume, except that strange hats were frequently worn. Sometimes my mother folded them out of typing paper, and they looked like boats.

We were also encouraged to come up with our own hats to enter into the spirit of the occasion. This meant using rolls and rolls of tinfoil, since as children we didn't have the contacts in the garment industry that we do now. Some of the styles were:

Viking Horned Helmet with Play-Doh Horns [favored by Larry]

Larry was fascinated with Norse mythology and tinfoil. He used to make himself tinfoil hammers like the one sported by the comic-book version of the god Thor. He enjoyed hitting people and things with this hammer when he became excited. In fact, after I told him I was writing this book, I instinctively ducked.

Cub Scout Cap with the Brim Cut Off and Turned into a Tinfoil Spiked Crown (favored by Danny)

Danny hated being in the Cub Scouts and enjoyed vandalizing his uniform. There wasn't that much to it. Let's move on.

Pointy-Topped Single-Spiked Dunce Cap (favored by Danny and Larry to force Mark to wear against his will)

Hey, Mark was the youngest and the smallest. As the Greek historian Thucydides wrote, "The strong do as they will, and the weak suffer what they must." As true today with American preteens as it was with warring Greek city-states. Mark on other occasions was zipped in a suitcase and rolled down the stairs, made to stand in the fire-place and told "Mommy says that's your new room," told he was adopted and could be sent back at any moment, and woken up at 4:00 A.M. and told it was on the radio that a nuclear war was starting and we were all going to die. He has never thanked me for these character-building exercises that made him what he is today. You're welcome, Mark.

THE Fuck Fascism SIGN

LIKE A DWINDLING number of patriotic Americans, our father is against fascism. To show his love for the freedoms we may enjoy for a little longer as Americans, including the freedom to make up holidays that would've got you disappeared in a fascist state like Mussolini's Italy, he poured out this feeling on a sign that read, obviously:

Fuck Facism!

This lovingly hand-crafted sign was scribbled in green ink on a piece of cardboard, which had been torn off a card-board box that once had held rosebushes bought at a local plant nursery. It was placed on the mantelpiece in the dining room, over the fireplace.

It would change from year to year because our mother hated it, finding its sentiment admirable but its phrasing vulgar, and so she would hide or destroy it after every Fes-tivus. So one year my dad gave in, and the sign read:

Screw Facism!

This didn't have quite the same bite as the original, so we went back to the R-rated version the next year.

THE AMERICAN FLAG

As PART OF the Festivus celebration, Dad would hang out Old Glory on the pole mounted on the upstairs porch. However, he also did this on other days as well: the Fourth of July and Memorial Day of course, but also:

Birthdays
Wedding anniversaries
The anniversary of Richard Nixon's resignation
Thanksgiving
Days when good report cards were brought home
After an exceptionally good meal
When he realized his son Mark wasn't gay

Note: This last one requires explaining. So here it is. As a practical joke, Danny and Larry convinced Dad that Mark, who was about sixteen at the time, was gay. The joke went even better than planned, as we were unable to unconvince him of this later. So he went out of his way to be "supportive" of Mark, but whenever Mark had a male friend over he couldn't look him in the eye. It was hilarious.

In any case, during the rich Golden Age of Festivus, a period that lasted from about 1975–85, once we came home from school to the candlelit, oddly decorated house, changed, and my mom finished cooking, the celebration would begin. Initially we would gather in the dining room, and the rough order of events was as follows:

The Poem of Festivus
The Music of Festivus
The Festivus Dinner and Festivus Gifts

Listening to Old Festivus Tapes and Making a New Festivus Tape

We will proceed to discuss each component in turn. If you skipped ahead, this will all make even less sense than it does already, if such a thing is possible.

THE POEM
OF FESTIVUS

There were many poems written specifically for each Festivus, some about what had happened to each of us during the year, and some that were just plain silliness. But there was a special Poem of Festivus that kicked off each holiday. After consulting the tapes, we have found it went like this:

Festivus

At Festivus, that time of year
When clock and bag are signs of cheer
And mystery of life is clear
Then come we all together here
To sing of love, and never fear.

In winter, nineteen sixty-two
He did not know what he could do
Until a clock had shown the way
And after that, lest more he stray,
A bag accepted made the day

Then children came here, one, two, three,
Each more keen and fine to see,

And each one filled with Mystery.
To which we sing, each Festivus,
Which we hold for the Rest Of Us.

Now let's go line by line, and see if I can break it down:

At Festivus, that time of year
Like I said, it wasn't any one time of year.

When clock and bag are signs of cheer
Like I said, I don't know what they're signs of. It's possible that it's cheer. It's just as possible that it's Cheer detergent.

And mystery of life is clear
If it's clear, why is it a mystery? Or does this mean at Festivus, it's clear that life is mysterious? The line itself remains a mystery, like the Rosary, or how I managed to trick a reputable publishing house into paying me for this.

Then come we all together here
To sing of love, and never fear.
We did do a lot of singing at Festivus, around the dinner table and into the tape recorder. However, the songs were rarely songs of love or fear, but generally just songs of extreme peculiarity.

In winter, nineteen sixty-two
He did not know what he could do
Until a clock had shown the way
This sounds like Dad didn't learn to tell time till he was in his thirties. Conceivable, but unlikely.

And after that, lest more he stray,
A bag accepted made the day

> This really sounds like my Dad was buying drugs, but that could not possibly be the case. His hatred of drugs is only exceeded by his ignorance of them. Until recently, I'm pretty sure he believed people shot marijuana into their veins with needles.

Then children came here, one, two, three,
Each more keen and fine to see,

> This sounds like he liked each child better than the one who came before. That is, Mark was his favorite, followed by Larry, with Danny in last place. This, too, is not the case. He did not have a permanent favorite among us. His preferences were updated on an hourly basis. As of press time, the rankings are:
>
> 1) Larry
> 2) Danny and Mark (tie)

And each one filled with Mystery.
To which we sing, each Festivus,
Which we hold for the Rest Of Us.

> This refers to the living. Most Festivi, there was a section when we shared memories of those family members who had passed away. Or, possibly, it refers to those cave-dwelling control-group siblings.

THE MUSIC
OF FESTIVUS

MUSIC WASN'T REALLY a discrete section of Festivus unto itself; rather, it was woven throughout all aspects of the holiday, like, oh, something you weave. Yarn? String? In any case, music played a large role in our home when we were children.

Larry was really good on the violin till he got bored with it, and he makes his living playing piano to this day. Danny was incompetent at piano, worse at clarinet, but then started playing a gigantic string bass, and was actually getting good. But he got tired of lugging it around on the school bus and quit when he tripped and fell down a flight of stairs, riding it like a sled. Mark was good at the piano but got bored with it. All three of us did those ridiculous high school musicals that are an excuse for cast parties where kids lose their virginity on someone's parents' roof. Our mother played the piano from an early age, and our father has sung all his life, sometimes on public transportation.

As a result of all this, Festivus was full of music, at the dinner table and into the tape recorder. Many songs were show tunes, arias from operas, old Irish songs, and in the late seventies, at Danny's insistence, the hits of Donna Summer. There were also far stranger songs and pieces of music that Dad made up. In the latter category, here are two of the more enduring Festivus favorites:

THE BIRD-AND-DUCK CHORUS

CAME TO BE a part of both the meal and the tape recording. It consisted of our father whistling—as the "bird," and his three sons making quacking noises into their fists—as the "ducks," all this as his wife "rolled her eyes." It was whistled and quacked to a tune called the "Merlitons" from the *Nutcracker Suite.*

Music by
PETER ILYICH TCHAIKOWSKY

Festivus Song #2: Bird And Duck Chorus
(after *The Nutcracker Suite*, Act 2: "The Merlitons")

It originated as something to be whistle-quacked as a long car trip neared its destination: when we were going on vacation, visiting a relative, and so on. If there was slow traffic and the windows were open, it provided quite a show for other drivers.

DEINE SCHWEINE (YOUR PIG)

WAS WRITTEN BY our dad, and supposedly intended to be a mnemonic device to help us remember German vocabulary. We bought this for a while: our folks had signed up all three of us for German language lessons at the local German cultural center, where we were the only non-German children and were looked on as freaks or spies. And so this song became a part of the Festivus celebration: it was often sung at the Festivus dinner table, and/or into the Festivus tape recorder. But on closer examination of the lyrics, it is revealed for what it is: a twisted nightmare out of the brothers Grimm, set to the melody of Richard Stauss's opera *Ariadne auf Naxos.*

Deine schweine ist kleine
Your pig is small

Und meine ist gross
And mine is large

Und schwarz und harmlos
And black and harmless

Here is it rendered into musical notation by Larry.

O'Keefe Festivus Book

Music by RICHARD STRAUSS
Lyrics by DANIEL O'KEEFE

Festivus Song #1: Deine Schweine
(after *Ariadne Auf Naxos*, Richard Strauss)

This is clearly an off-key warning shot fired in German over the increasingly rebellious bows of three young boys. However, it could also be seen as a patriarch reasserting his symbolic authority—vested in his "large, black pig," yet reassuring his family that it will be used fairly—his pig may be frightening, but it is "harmless" to those in his family, perhaps intended more for defense of the family unit against outside threats than for dominating his wife and children.

On the other hand, maybe it's just fuckin' nuts.

We asked an actual professional for his expert opinion of this little song. Dr. Herman Reinman is a board-certified psychiatrist with thirty-some years of experience treating troubled people in a suburb of Los Angeles. He is certainly not a fictional construct whose mouth we've put words in because we couldn't get any self-respecting shrink to analyze this weird song.

DANNY: So, what do you think?

DR. R: It's very interesting.

DANNY: Is that shrink-speak for "fuckin' nuts?"

DR. R: I wouldn't characterize it that way.

DANNY: How would you characterize it?

DR. R: Obviously there is a strong sexual subtext. The symbology is so apparent as to scarcely require explaining.

DANNY: Man, that's a lot of fancy words.

DR. R: Alright, I believe most professionals would say the "pig" in the song referred to the male genitalia. And using the word *pig* in this way could be said to display a disgust with sexuality itself. Pigs are dirty, sex is dirty, that kind of thing.

DANNY: Pigs are actually very clean animals.

DR. R: I wasn't aware of that.

DANNY: Yeah, they get a bad rap. I saw it on the nature channel. They're also very smart, like dolphins.

DR. R: Huh. Well, I think the song is a coded assertion of paternal authority, accompanied by an assurance that the authority will not be misused, that it is harmless to the members of the family unit. It's unusual, but pretty straightforwardly Oedipal.

DANNY: Doc, would you mind dangling me upside down by my feet to see if I'm schizophrenic?

DR. R: I have to go.

(He leaves.)

Birds, ducks, and pigs of any color and size notwith-standing, the true theme song of Festivus lies elsewhere. It is a ballad about an Irish terrorist from the "Wolfe Tone" Rebellion of 1798, who is hanged by the British for refus-ing to give up the other members of his cell. And it is called:

Kevin Barry

In Mountjoy Jail one Monday morning,
High upon the gallows tree,
Kevin Barry gave his young life
For the cause of liberty . . .

This is a beloved old Irish tune, and like most old Irish tunes, is about that island's fight for freedom from English domination. Of course, Kevin Barry may have been little bet-ter than today's drugs-and-arms-dealing IRA dirtbags, but such ambiguities never bothered our father, who loved this song above all others and sang it before, during, and espe-cially after Festivus, because its gorgeous and mournful waltz melody was ideal after a long evening of celebrations and recriminations, and afterward a fitting accompaniment for trudging upstairs to the library to read impenetrable German philosophy while drinking crappy American beer.

Just before he reached the hangman,
In his dreary prison cell,
British soldiers tortured Barry
Just because he would not tell . . .

At this point our dad would lean into the melody with extra brio and the thickening Irish brogue of his grand-father, pronouncing the word "the" with two syllables as the tune rose:

. . . Thu-huh names of his companions,
Sartin things they wished to know:
"Turn informer or we'll kill you!"
Kevin bravely answered: No.

This ballad combines all the darker elements of Festivus in one sweaty knot: celebration of injustices past, the sense of being surrounded by enemies, a brave yet retarded refusal to ever cooperate with anyone, a vague affinity with Catholic martyrdom stories, fierce nationalism, and the worship of death. And such a pretty tune!

Songs From Festivus

Kevin Barry

Traditional
arr. Daniel O'Keefe

1. In Mount-joy Jail one Sun-day morn-in', high up - on the gal-lows tree, Kev-in Bar-ry gave his young life For the cause of li-ber - ty. Just a lad of eigh-teen sum-mers, Yet there's no one can de - ny, As he walked to death that morn-in', Kev-in held his head on high.

2. Just before he faced the hangman,
In his dreary prison cell,
British soldiers tortured Barry
Just because he would not tell
The names of his companions,
Certain things they wished to know:
"Turn informer or we'll kill you!"
Kevin bravely answered, "No."

3. Calmly standing to attention,
While he bade his last farewell
To his broken hearted mother
Whose sad grief no one can tell.
For the cause he proudly cherished
This sad parting had to be;
Then to death he walked on smiling,
That old Ireland might be free.

4. Another martyr for old Ireland;
Another murder for the crown,
Whose brutal laws may kill the Irish
But can't keep their spirit down.
Lads like Barry are no cowards,
From the foe they will not fly.
Lads like Barry will free Ireland;
For her sake they'll live and die.

Music was always present in our household, but money did not always accompany it. Dad bought a piano, but we couldn't tune it. Larry finally quit piano lessons after a few years when Dad began hinting that we wouldn't be able to afford luxuries like lessons when the U.S. economy collapsed in five weeks, our savings became worthless, and we'd be burning useless dollars to stay warm as looters stripped our copper plumbing. But mostly Larry quit because the piano keys were splintery and cut his fingers. He has real delicate fingers. It's very masculine.

We played records on a stereo with high-tech-looking buttons and lights that weren't really lights, but were actually painted on. When the needle on its record player wore out, rather than replace it we taped pennies to the arm to weigh it down and grind a few more years out of it. And that record player was always playing some warped LP from my dad's terrifying collection. During Festivus dinner, any or all of the following would be hauled out and played in the background to delight us again:

Orfeo ed Eurydice by Gluck: This opera chronicles Orpheus' journey into hell to rescue his wife, which fails. Beautiful, but not exactly cheerful.

Ariadne auf Naxos by Strauss: This opera is about a woman abandoned on an island by her lover, the God Apollo. Lovely, but again, kind of depressing.

Honeymoon In Rome: Jaunty Italian pop tunes from the sixties, featuring accordion and that apex of sixties masculine cool, the vibraphone. With some cheerfully oily, cut-rate Dean Martin crooning in Eye-talian, accompanied by leering backup singers whose voices were sped up like Alvin and the Chipmunks. *I am not kidding.*

Sylvie Vartan, My Boyfriend's Back: A French pop tart of the fifties. In her mouth, songs like "Alley-Oop" and "My Boyfriend's Back" sounded like the toothless come-ons of a Parisian whore.

Four Saints In Three Acts and *In Circles:* The fractured and kaleidoscopic work of Gertrude Stein ("Rose is a rose is a rose," "Pigeons on the grass, alas") set to music. Apparently these were two works of musical genius from composers like Virgil Thompson. To us at the time, it sounded like a hundred-foot tall baby stomping on a symphony orchestra, smashing the instruments, splattering the players and the choir, and then taking a dump on the kettledrum.

From Berlin With Love: German pop tunes of the late fifties, less jaunty, mostly accordion, no vibraphone. Usually no vocals, either. Played during the tapings. A little ominous sounding, and a sign that the accumulated bile of the year was about to explode in a flood.

I-Feel-Like-I'm-Fixin'-To-Die by Country Joe and the Fish. This one Larry found in Dad's collection. He always asked him to play it, but Dad hated it, calling it the ravings of dirty hippies. He was right: the hippies on the cover were among the dirtiest ever seen. Each member of the Fish was dressed uniquely: a wizard in Dungeons and Dragons robes, a circus strongman, a caveman in furs gnawing a bone. They resembled a proto-Village People who sang about

Nixon and LSD instead of sodomy. They sang jaunty lyrics like "be the first ones on your block to have your boy come home in a box!" My dad hated Nixon, but he hated hippies and wizards, too, so Larry asked, "if they're so dirty and nasty, why do you still have this album?" His answer: "To keep an eye on them."

After dinner we'd retire upstairs, and sing songs from shows or chorus concerts that we had performed at school. Always unaccompanied, we'd start out enthusiastic and then gradually lose our enthusiasm as we realized once again just how lonely we sounded. Over the years our thin and high voices gave way to our thin and cracking voices, and then to more sullen muttering. Then we stopped singing at all and would just answer in our robotic, maladjusted, adolescent monotones. Listen to all the tapes in sequence and it sounds like a children's opera written by Philip Glass, or the score of one of those David Cronenberg thrillers where Jeremy Irons goes crazy and mutilates identical twins.

Our dad also liked to make up songlike chants specifically for the tape recorder, and we would all then intone the slogans he had devised. The first time we got a real glimpse into the pain of being an adult was when Dad made us repeat the chant "Daddy's on a treadmill, see Daddy run" about five hundred times, referring to his grueling job. We found ourselves feeling sorry for him, fighting back tears, wishing for British soldiers to come hang us all and end the evening.

After the songs died away and the taping ended, we would all straggle away, and my dad would bring out the last record of the evening; the post-Festivus music. It was usually *Stardust*, by Willie Nelson, that LP-length dark night of the soul, in which Willie would mumble the classic ballads of the big-band era over a whispering accompaniment of guitar, piano, organ, harmonica and one really stoned drummer. You haven't questioned your life until you've heard Willie Nelson intone "Georgia On My Mind" or "Don't Get Around Much Anymore" or, saddest of all, "Unchained Melody."

Many of you know that song from the uplifting quasi-gospel version from the movie *Ghost*, but I first heard it from Willie, who clearly recorded it in a cloud of doobie smoke, bourbon vapor, and regret. This is what our dad would end the evening with. Either that or "Kevin Barry."

Another important piece of music, as it applies to Festivus is *Irish Songs of Freedom*. If you can find this album, please notify Larry. He's obsessed with it. This album is the Holy Grail for him. Danny once brought it to a party in high school and forgot it there, and Larry has literally cursed him over this ever since. "You frickin' no-account Limerick trash can whore!" is one of the politer things he has actually called him and will continue to call him. It remains unclear why Danny thought bringing a record of Irish death ballads to a high school party would help him with the chicks.

Now, *Irish Songs Of Freedom* is just one guy and his guitar, but it's the most haunting thing you'll ever hear.

> *Oh Paddy dear, and did ye hear*
> *The news that's going round?*
> *The shamrock is forbid by law*
> *To grow on Irish ground.*

That's from "The Wearin' of the Green," about how the British would shoot people wearing green, because it was a sign of solidarity with the rebels.

All around me hat I wear a three-colored ribbon,
All around me hat until death comes to me,
And if anybody asks me why I'm wearing that ribbon,
It's all for my true love,
I never more shall see.

That's "The Three-Colored Ribbon," about a woman missing her IRA boyfriend, who may or may not have been shot yet. Since she's wearing green she's either very brave or the local Brits are all colorblind and she's convinced them it's orange.

These songs were all political, and not a few of them were celebrations of raids gone wrong or noble young men walking to certain death. In "The Croppy Boy," a young Irish patriot boy goes to confession and reveals his participation in an IRA raid gone wrong. But lo and behold, the priest is actually a British soldier in disguise, and the Croppy Boy is sent away to be hung on a warship in the river! You can't frickin' win.

And then there's "Kevin Barry." Near the end of the song, Kevin's mother comes and pleads for his life as he stands on the gallows, but Kevin waves her off and swings for Ireland, no doubt nobly crapping his heroic pants, as one does when hanged.

Men like Barry are no cowards,
From the foe they will not fly.
Men like Barry will free Ireland,
For her sake they live and die.

And that was part of the magic of Festivus: the song was so beautiful and compelling that we all assumed we'd have to die for Ireland too, at some point. None of us ever thought to ask Dad if Ireland was free yet.

FESTIVUS DINNER AND GIFTS

estivus dinner was almost a holiday within a holiday. In some ways it resembled and may have been partly based on the medieval "Feast of Fools." Now, that holiday was designed to allow the peasant and mercantile classes to let off a little steam, so they didn't rise up and kill their feudal overlords. The *Catholic Encyclopedia* calls it, "a celebration marked by much license and buffoonery, which in many parts of Europe, and particularly in France, during the later middle ages took place every year on or about the feast of the Circumcision (January first). It was known by many names—*festum fatuorum, festum stultorum, festum hypodiaconorum*, to notice only some Latin variants—and it is difficult, if not quite impossible, to distinguish it from certain other similar celebrations, such, for example, as the Feast of Asses . . ." For this one day in a year, which had its origin in the Roman holiday of Saturnalia (as opposed to the *Roman Holiday* of Audrey Hepburn), lords dressed as commoners and vice versa. There was great gluttony, drunkenness, revelry, and a general relaxing of the rules: people low down on the social scale might be allowed to openly make fun of the higher-ups, in songs, skits, and unflattering impressions.

Elements of this medieval feast seem to have made their way into the dinner portion of Festivus. For like those long-dead, shit-covered peasants in those weird, furry, middle-agey caps with earflaps, we were allowed (if not encouraged) at this one dinner to openly mock Dad's politics, Mom's cooking, the time Mark crapped his pants on a long car ride to Vermont, the time Danny accidentally peed in a doctor's face as a baby, the way Larry's home-made haircut made him look like a girl, and so on. Also, the plate licking that our father favored, but our mother forbade, was grudgingly permitted at this particular meal. And since it would have been hypocritical to let only one person flout the laws of table manners and common decency, *all* of us were free to:

Lick plates

Talk with our mouths full

Toss half-chewed things we didn't like under the table

Interrupt our parents and each other

Swear (up to a point)

Eat in any order we chose (for instance, have pie first)

Do nasty impressions of each other

While these were grudgingly permitted, they were not encouraged, and occasionally made our mother (who was raised in a civilized fashion) very angry. Only the nasty impressions of each other have survived to this day. Occasionally, if all three of us are annoyed enough at each other, Danny will start talking in a hostile, weird voice that's supposed to be Mark; Mark will start jabbering in a breezily arrogant, affected, effeminate voice that's supposed to be

Larry; and Larry will begin mumbling in a depressed, robotic monotone that's supposed to be Danny. We'll all start mocking each other *as* each other, louder and louder, and it sounds like pudding night in an insane asylum.

Regarding the food that was eaten at Festivus dinner, before we were born it was turkey. When Festivus was revived, it again started out as a turkey dinner, because turkey is cheap compared to most other kinds of meat. But as the years passed and Dad advanced at work, it became ham, beef stew, and finally we settled on lamb chops. My mother always cooked it, whatever it was, along with mashed potatoes, gravy, beans, and a pecan pie for dessert. For *your* Festivus celebration, here are some actual Festivus recipes by our actual mother, Deborah O'Keefe:

A FESTIVUS MEAL

★

No-Cream Cream of Chicken Soup

Make broth and cook chicken by putting chicken parts (with bones) in a big pot—maybe 2 chicken breasts and 4 leg-and-thigh pieces, or some such combination. Add a lot of water (more than enough to cover pieces), a sliced onion, a peeled sliced carrot, a bay leaf; bring to a boil, then turn down to a simmer; skim off the scummy stuff that forms on top. Simmer uncovered about an hour; cool. Remove the chicken parts and cut up the good meat into small pieces, discarding bones and gristly bits. Strain the remaining broth through a big strainer to get rid of yucky material.

In another pot melt 4 tablespoons butter; stir in 3/4 cup flour. A little at a time, whisk in 8 cups of the broth, stirring constantly so it stays smooth. (This is like the process of making white sauce or gravy.) Add 1 onion, 2 leeks (or a second onion), and 2 stalks celery, all chopped rather fine—this time the vegetables will *not* be strained out. Add some chopped parsley, and salt and pepper to taste. Simmer 30 minutes, stirring occasionally.

To get the consistency you want, add some milk after the simmering (or heavy cream if you want it richer) or else just use the soup as is. Add the chicken pieces and reheat. If you want rice in the soup, add some for the last 20 minutes of the simmering. I'm not sure how much—if you used 8 cups of broth for the liquid, maybe ¾ cup rice? If you prefer a noodle soup, add pasta for the last 10 minutes of the simmering. If you want mushrooms in it, sauté them before putting them in the soup at the end. If you want a bit of carrot, grate some into the soup for the last 5 minutes of simmering. Or you can cook some washed spinach in water for a few minutes, then chop or puree and drain, then add to the soup at the end, stirring and reheating briefly.

SERVES ABOUT 6.

★

Beef Stew from Galena, Illinois

USE ABOUT 2 pounds of beef-chuck or round or whatever a butcher tells you is good. Amounts don't matter in this stew; just put in an amount of meat and a proportion of vegetables that seem right. Either order the meat cut in pieces or cut it yourself, into half-inch chunks. Pat them dry with paper towels and sprinkle with salt and paper. Roll pieces in flour and shake off excess flour, then brown them in a big pot with a little oil heated in the bottom along with a few slices of onion. Only brown one layer of pieces at a time; then remove to a plate while you do another layer. If you do too many at once, the pieces become gray and slimy and don't get nice and brown and crisp.

When all the meat is browned, put it back in the pot. Add enough water so that it more than covers the meat. You can throw in a bouillon cube or two for extra flavor, but it's not essential. Add an onion, chopped up but in biggish pieces, and a peeled carrot cut in pieces. Also, add 2 bay leaves and contents of a 16-ounce can of stewed tomatoes, including the juice. This will look unpleasant, but the tomatoes dissolve and add a great flavor. Bring pot to a boil then turn down to a simmer and cover pot. Simmer until meat is fairly tender (approximately 1½ hours). Don't let the broth boil down too much—add more water if necessary. But if the broth seems too watery, you can remove the cover and turn up the heat a bit, to thicken the broth a little.

Now add the real, final vegetables—the onion and carrot used already just give flavor to the meat, and they're cooked so long they disintegrate. Put in potatoes and carrots peeled and cut to the same size as the meat pieces. Use whatever amount you want: taste or economy may influence whether you like meat or vegetables to predominate. If you like that sort of thing, include a turnip or two. Maybe some green beans. It's good to add a splash of wine, either red or white. Now simmer the stew, covered, until the vegetables are soft but not totally squashy, an hour or less. Adjust the seasoning to taste. Serve with green salad and good bread. It's even better the second day.

SERVES ABOUT 6.

★

"Three of a Kind" Ice Cream

This is my grandmother's recipe (Harriet Webb Crawford). My mother, born in 1902, had it often as a child. My mother submitted this to a little cookbook put out by St. Francis Church in Stamford, Connecticut, in 1962. She was horrified when her handwritten instruction to use "mashed bananas" appeared as "washed bananas." I had always told her her lowercase *m*'s looked like *w*'s, and I was right. The recipe is really good, very fresh-tasting but also rich.

The tradition is to call this three of a kind, and to use three of each ingredient. But that makes a very big batch— it fills three old-type ice-trays.

Instead I usually make batches of one or two of each ingredient.

Freeze it in any kind of container that is freezable, probably plastic.

> *3 ripe, mashed bananas*
> *juice of 3 oranges*
> *juice of 3 lemons*
> *3 cups sugar*
> *3 cups heavy cream*
> *3 cups water*

Mix all together in a large bowl—freeze—stirring occasionally. If you don't stir it as it freezes, it will separate a little bit, with the creamy part tending to the bottom and the fruit juice to the top. But if you stir it, it will be smooth and lovely.

Thanks, Mom.

THE FESTIVUS TABLE

NOW, THE TABLE the Festivus meal was served on would be decorated with chocolate kisses and other candies, but also odd little figurines and tchotchkes of animals. Because we ate by candlelight, once in a while someone bit into a small ceramic frog or something, thinking it was candy, and cracked a tooth. Also on the table were small pots of Play-Doh, one by each place setting. During dinner we were not only expected to eat and keep up our end of the conversation, but also to mold our individual Play-Doh into an object of some kind. This was a contest, and my mother would judge who the winner was; for instance who molded the best clay frog to replace the bitten ceramic one. The winner received nothing but the resentment of the losers, an important life lesson that has not been lost on us, and should not be lost on you.

During dinner was when we exchanged and opened gifts. Just a few, not a huge haul like Christmas or Hanukkah. Us boys generally wrapped up household items in wrapping paper and presented them to our parents and each other: Mark liked wrapping up rolls of toilet paper; Larry was fond of forks and knives; and Danny favored either books that Dad was in the middle of reading, or rocks and sticks from the yard.

The parent-to-child gifts were also quite often joke gifts. We think Mom once gave Mark a fake plastic camera that squirted water. But the only *surviving* Festivus gift is and was both amusing and educational: a small metal wastebasket given to Danny, studded with pictures of all the presidents of the United States up till then. Since he was president at the time, Richard Nixon occupied the place of honor in the middle, and his picture was bigger.

The Presidential Trash Can

This president can is also where Danny threw up the first time he got drunk, when as a junior in high school he drank a bottle of something called "bourbon champagne" that had a picture of a duck on the bottle. It has been cleaned since then, but not often.

THE
FESTIVUS TAPES

These are the centerpiece of the holiday. Tapes survive from 1975 to 1991, with only 1978 and 1979
missing. It is a strong possibility that Danny taped over
them with Donna Summer's double album *On the Radio*.
The listening to and the making of these tapes took up the
majority of the celebration, and it was treated with the
greatest solemnity. There was always a distinct feeling that
we were in fact making the tapes as a secret testament of
our trials and tribulations, like French partisans scratch-
ing messages on the walls of the attic where they were hid-
ing from the Nazis. Or as a record that aliens would find
one day far in the future, while picking through the nuclear
rubble of our civilization. And the possibility of having to
hide from the government in the attic and nuclear annihi-
lation were topics that were actually discussed at our dinner table, and not just on Festivus, either.

Anyway, after Festivus dinner we would head up to the
living room with the remnants of our drinks and dessert,
and listen to the tapes of previous years. Then Dad would
pop a new Maxell into his 1969-model Dictaphone, and
we'd make a new tape, to chronicle our life as a family over

that year. Coached by our father, we would speak, sing, laugh, cry, and make odd noises into the little black box, celebrating and bitching about the family's past year.

These tapes generally started with the statement of the theme of that year's Festivus. The statement of a theme for the year began with the 1976 Festivus. These themes were frequently alarming and gloomy.

YEAR—THEME

1976—Are We Scared? Yes!

1977—Are We Depressed? Yes!

1978—Unknown: Tape has been lost

1979—This year there seem to have been multiple themes. Since 1978 and 1979 are lost, we only know this because the previous year's themes are mentioned on the 1980 tape. Anyway, 1979's themes were:

Coraggio! (that's Italian for "Courage!")
Don't Give Up the Ship!
Overcome Fellacity!

Fellacity is not a word. An online dictionary search gave up the following:
Sorry, no dictionaries indexed in the selected category contain the word *fellacity*.
Perhaps you meant:

felicity (found in 23 dictionaries)
feracity (found in 6 dictionaries)
facility (found in 30 dictionaries)
fall city (found in 3 dictionaries)
felicita (found in 3 dictionaries)
fayalite (found in 9 dictionaries)
fecalith (found in 7 dictionaries)
fireclay (found in 11 dictionaries)
focillate (found in 5 dictionaries)
facelift (found in 10 dictionaries)

Incidentally, according to the same online dictionary, the meaning of *fecalith* is "a stony mass of dried feces.")

1980—This year, almost all family members had his or her own theme assigned to him or her.

Dad's Theme: (Are We) Too Easily Made Glad?
Larry's Theme: What . . . Happen . . . Next?
Mom's Theme: Can We Top This?
Danny's Theme: Are We Pushovers?
Mark's Theme: (Did not get a theme.)

1981—Again, this year brought multiple themes.
Let's Be Serious!
Let's Try to Do Better!
Let's Use Our Talents!
Let's Make Some Changes!

1982—Again, multiple themes.
Which Way Is Up?
What . . . Happen . . . Next? (again)
Disgustipated, but Not Humiligrated!

1983—Cope! or You Gotta Cope, Man!
(This theme was repeated in the following beatnik-style chant: "You gotta cope, man. Don't be a dope, man.")

1984—Are We Getting Along, or Are We Getting On?

1985—No theme

1986—Not that We *Shall* Be Serious, but that We *Grow* Serious

1987—Life . . . Is Like a Fountain
This refers to an old joke our dad told us when we were young. It goes like this:

> A young man named Fred works as a librarian. One day, he wonders, what is the meaning of life? This question begins to occupy all his thoughts. He begins to slack off at work. Eventually, he gets fired, and all he does is sit around the house, thinking about the meaning of life. Soon, his wife leaves him. But all he can do is think about the meaning of life. In a few months, he gets evicted for nonpayment of rent, but all he can think about is the meaning of life.

As Fred lives on the street, he hears rumors of a wise man in Tibet who knows the meaning of life. Desperate to know, Fred scrapes together some cash and buys a plane ticket to Tibet. In Tibet, he searches for this wise man, and learns that he lives in a cave at the peak of a remote, dangerous mountain.

Fred spends his last penny on a yak to help him get up this mountain. As they climb, the cruel winds and bitter snows tear at them every step of the way. Halfway up the mountain, the yak dies, but Fred soldiers on. He *has* to know the meaning of life. At this point, Fred is on his hands and knees, half dead from cold and exhaustion. With his last ounce of strength, he manages to make it to the top and sees a tiny cave. Somehow, he's able to haul himself, barely clinging to life, into this cave. There he sees before him a small, white-haired man sitting by a fire. Fred forces the question he has traveled so far from his cracked, frostbitten lips: "Sir," says Fred, "I have traveled long and far to learn the meaning of life. I'm told you know what it is. I beg of you, share it with me." The old man pauses and softly says, "Life is like a fountain." Fred cannot believe his ears. That's it?

"That's it?" he says. "I lose my job, my wife, my money, my house, go broke flying here, I climb up this mountain, my yak dies, I'm half-dead, and all you can tell me is *life is like a fountain?*"

The old man looks puzzled and says, "You mean life is *not* like a fountain?"

1988—We'll See How It Goes!

1989—No theme

1990—We Can't Stop Singing!

1990 was also . . .

> The Secret Festivus
> Also called the "Hidden Festivus." We were unable to schedule a Festivus time that year, or maybe we refused to, so basically our dad hid a tape recorder around the house while we were home from college over a weekend, to capture our conversations, and whispered commentary into the machine as he taped it. Weird, huh?

1991—Io Triumphe!
> (Meaning, "I am triumphant!" "I kick ass!" "I rule!" or "I rock!" in some language or other.)

So: the themes follow a parabolic arc. The first themes deal with fear and depression, moving on to beleaguered statements of courage and exhortations not to abandon the metaphorical ship of our family, then to worries that our family was resting on its laurels, too easily pleased and couldn't top itself, then to the forced positivity of 1981's orgy of Let's Be! themes. Eventually a cautious optimism prevails with We'll See How It Goes, and then a previously unseen exuberance bursts through the clouds of gloom with We Can't Stop Singing! The themes concluded with an actual statement of triumph. This movement coincided with my parents' movement from being house-poor and saddled with three brats, all the way through to being relatively comfortable, with their offspring finally out of the damn house.

Now, as we sat around the tape recorder, after the theme was established, Dad would ask each family member to speak about his or her experiences over the past year or so, since the last Festivus. The triumphs, the tragedies, the small joys and sorrows. And yes, there certainly was an *airing of grievances*. In our father's case, this often had to do with the Kremlin-like internal politics of the *Reader's Digest* magazine, where he was an editor.

In my mother's case, this frequently took the form of complaining about the college students she taught expository and creative writing to: they were dirty, smelly, sullen, drug-addled jerks unwilling to learn and barely able to read. We children complained about being beaten at school, being stuffed into tight spaces at school, and not being listened to by teachers when we complained about being beaten and stuffed into tight spaces. But:

Just as much of the Festivus tape recordings was taken up with more pleasant memories. Trips and vacations we'd taken. Promotions, anniversaries, the visits of relatives, getting a new furnace so we didn't freeze to death in the New York winters. A tape recording might also contain Mark singing some song from a school play he was in; Larry having to recite something in Latin that he'd learned in Latin class; Danny triumphantly detailing how he escaped from behind a radiator at school after a beating and a stuffing; our father reliving the night Nixon was forced from office; or my mother talking nostalgically about the period before she was married.

But you can see for yourself. Here are transcriptions of some of the actual tapes we recorded back then. So, without further ado, here they are.

FESTIVUS 1976
OR: "ARE WE SCARED? YES!"

DAD: Testing for Festivus, testing for Festivus. This is another Festivus . . . (*dramatic pause*) . . . for the rest of us. This is the fourteenth annual anniversary of . . . you-know-what! (*We don't know.*) What kind of a year has it been? It has been a year in which Daddy wrote his crazy Ph.D. dissertation, which is thirteen times as long as it's supposed to be. It is a year with great changes at work, which may mean that we will not be at work much longer. It is a year in which all of the children have advanced in school and have been asked to join special programs. Danny went to Washington all by himself. (*To see our cousins who lived there. This is not* code *for, "he ran away."*)

Last year, all five of us went to Martha's Vineyard all by ourselves. We weren't scared! We are facing the future that may lie ahead with downright abandon! Are we scared? (*The question is repeated to the children, who have forgotten their cue.*)

DAD: Are we scared?

DANNY: No.

DAD: Are we scared?

LARRY: Yes!

DAD: I'm calling on Mommy, if she will stop trembling over there, to tell us how we have spent this Festivus!

MOM: This Festivus evening, we've had a big banquet of lamb chops and other good things, including chocolate kisses, everyone has given speeches and toasts and cheers for the family.

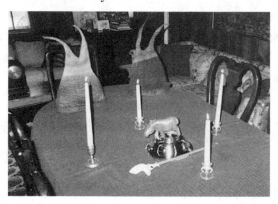

DAD: *(in a stagey, mock-terrified horror-movie voice)* And nobody's scared!

MARK: *(sincerely)* I'm scared.

DAD: We have played an interesting game at dinner, which is "What is the earliest thing you remember?" Danny, what is the earliest thing you remember?

DANNY: The earliest thing I remember is when Mom and me *(Danny must have got a very dirty look here, because our mother was a college English professor at the* *time, and speaking incorrectly was right up there with smearing poo on the walls, as far as no-nos went)* were going on a picnic with Penny *(Penny Stillinger, my mother's college roommate)*. Larry and Mark and Amy weren't born yet. *(Amy is Penny's younger daughter.)* Mom was spreading a cloth when I ran down into a shallow pond. I was—

DAD: *(interrupting)* Wa-wa-wa-wait! You went into a shallow pond? When was this? Come here, when was this?

MOM: Well, I never really told you.

DAD: Why, why didn't you tell me?

(By this point it's clear that while the memory is real, the outrage is being staged for our amusement. Or maybe it's a re-creation of earlier, real outrage.)

DAD: Where did this happen?

MOM: In Central Park.

DAD: In Central Park? You never told me? That's alright, we're not scared!

MARK: *(again, sincere)* I'm scared!

DAD: Larry, let's see if you don't have a higher-class memory than that. Larry, what is your earliest memory? When you came on the scene, maybe? When you came out?

MOM: Excuse me?

(It appears that here our father is asking his son if he remembers being born.)

LARRY: Well, it all started when my big brother, Danny O'Keefe, got this wonderful idea, but I didn't think it was so wonderful.

(Note: Larry, though seven, is for some reason speaking in a world-weary, campy-sarcastic tone like that of some transvestite cabaret singer in Berlin between the wars. This may be why in later years, Mark, in his show The O'Keefes *on the WB network, while keeping the names Danny and Mark O'Keefe intact, changed Larry to Lauren. Turning Larry into a girl, in effect. The running joke here has been that Larry is gay. After all, he writes musicals and wears brightly colored embroidered vests on occasion, and he also has a wife who's just a little too attractive, like he has something to prove. But anyway, back to Danny's wonderful idea.)*

DAD: When was this?

LARRY: *(a little too fabulous)* Well! It happened when Danny got the wonderful idea, and this is what he did. He piled—he put me in my crib, and he brought lots of, as many toys as he could pick up on top of me. Then my mother came in.

DAD: *(mock-terrified)* Wha-wha-wha when was this, when was this?

LARRY: *(shrugging, presumably)* Ehh. . . .

DAD: Debby, when was this?

MOM: Well, he wasn't quite a year old, but it didn't really hurt him.

DAD: What was it, pillows and furniture? When was this? I was in New York? I mean, what's been going on around here?

MOM: His head was a little bit dented, but it straightened out.

(It's still a little dented.)

DAD: We're not scared! Are we scared? Are we scared?

LARRY: Yes!

DAD: We're terrified! Now here we have little Mark, Mark is now four years old. Mark, what is your earliest memory?

MARK: Ahh . . . (*he makes a bird noise*) I wanna . . . think of another thing.

DAD: Alright, what was your earliest memory?

MARK: Borrrrrn!

DAD: What happened to you when you were just born, Mark?

MARK: *(inarticulate noise)*

DAD: Yes, that was good.

MARK: When we were in another thing, and we came home from (*deep breath*) shopping. And I was just walking slowly, and this car came running fast!

DAD: Actually, at dinner Mark told his earliest memory, and it was different. It was when Tricia took Larry and Danny *(Patricia was an old baby-sitter)* away to the zoo, and why is it, Mommy, that Mark especially remembers that day?

MOM: Because he was learning to use the toilet, and he went around all day without any pants on.

DAD: That was good. We're not frightened, are we? Are we frightened?

ALL: Yessssss!

DAD: Who knows what the future may bring? But there's one thing that cannot be taken away from us. And that's the past! We are now opening up the past, folks. So here are the wedding photos—hey, who are those kids?

(This refers to how young my parents looked on their wedding day, not that any of us children were already born, out of wedlock.)

DAD: Getting married! *(humming some weddingy song)* Bum bum bum, dum dum dum dum dum dum dum, bum bum bum bum—*(coughs)*

MOM: Who is that, boys? Who does that look like?

MARK: Daddy!

MOM: And who is that? Is that Mark?

MARK: No! I wasn't borm!

DAD: And there's Mommy, going off to the wedding. And there's Cricket, looking rather somber. *(Cricket is our aunt, my mother's sister.)*

MOM: *(annoyed, re: tape recorder)* Is this on?

DAD: It's on.

MOM: Well, maybe a little gloomy. And there is a picture of Mommy—

LARRY: What does gloomy mean?

MOM: —going off to get married—

DAD: She looks frightened!

MOM: —and Mommy has kind of a . . . kind of a sick look on her face, except nobody knows why she looks sick.

DAD: They drugged her! They drugged her and took her off! Has to be, she's marrying an Irishman! Now here is the wedding reception. Everybody is going through the line, saying, *(in a bad imitation of the Connecticut WASP accent of my mother's family)* "Hello there. Hello there, Mrs. O'Keefe. Congratulations." *(looking at photo)* I think that's *(our cousin)* Richard Ball *(then, "as" my cousin, in a squeaky voice)* "Of course I'm Richard Ball! Who do you think I am?"

MOM: I'd like to comment on one picture. There is a picture of Mommy at the wedding. Richard Ball is looking at her. She is looking at Richard Ball with an astonished look on her face. She is grasping her stomach as if in horror at what she sees in her future. *(giggles)*

DAD: Uh-oh. There's a baby in your future. Let's look at another picture.

DAD: Here are the bachelors.

LARRY: I think they look like butlers.

DAD: They look like butlers, don't they. One of them is almost seven feet tall; that's Charlie Slack. *(A friend of our dad's from high school.)* Another of them is under four feet tall; that's Charlie Ramond.

DAD: That's right. These were called my best men, or my ushers.

MARK: *(sounding like he's just eaten a pound of sugar)* Usherrrrs!

DAD: That's right, ushers. As we advance into the future that lies ahead, all of us have taken this year some Festivus vows, and all of us have given a Festivus speech. Here is my Festivus speech. *(shouted)* Finish graduate school! Danny, what is your motto for the next year?

DANNY: *(sounding like a retarded Catskills comic of the 1950s)* Make it good! Dah, dah dah, dah dah dah!

THE 1975 FESTIVUS POEM

"*AT* Festivus, that time of year . . ." begins nearly every tape we looked at. However, the 1975 Festivus, it seems, had a different poem:

FESTIVUS '75

Albertine is disparu
But then, she was a friend to you.

Today I am an oldish crock
But I was saved once by a clock

And lest I should then start to sag
You followed it up with your bag.

Other than the fact that my mother had a friend named Albertine who moved to Chicago and so might be said to be "disparu" or lost, this one defies interpretation. If you, reader, have any theories as to what it might mean . . . keep it to yourself. Or contact our editor, Michelle Howry, at Perigee Books. Because of her busy schedule, the best time to contact her at home is around 4.00 A.M., before the rush starts.

DAD: Larry, come and give your Festivus speech. Larry, what happened when the toys were piled on top of you? How did you get out?

LARRY: *(bad-movie tough guy)* Lemme tell you. *(suddenly effeminate)* My mother came in and said "Where's Larry?" And then Danny just said, *(raspberry sound)*. And then suddenly, boop! A foot stuck out, from the toys in my crib. Me!

DAD: That was you! That's how we knew where you were.

LARRY: *(dramatically)* That's who was in there!

DAD: *(melodramatically)* And you grew up straight and fine! Despite this terrible trauma at an early age.

(Larry in fact has poor posture.)

LARRY: Hey, listen, you're crazy.

(Sound of Danny torturing Mark, and Mark objecting)

LARRY: My back is like spaghetti.

(Dad appears to put a stop to Danny torturing Mark. The tape is stopped and restarted.)

DAD: Larry, what is your motto for the future?

LARRY: Gimme an *L*!

DAD: *L!*

LARRY: Gimme an *I*!

DAD: *(and Mom, who has clearly been made to join in)*: *I!*

LARRY: Gimme an *F*!

DAD AND MOM: *F!*

LARRY: Gimme an *E!*

DAD AND MOM: *E!*

LARRY: What does it spell?

ALL: *Life!*

LARRY: Yessiree!

(I don't have any idea what that means. "Life" is a word, not a motto.)

DAD: Hurray!

DANNY: And the walls came tumbling down!

DAD: *(alarmed)* What's this with the walls?

(The tape cuts out, then is turned back on.)

DAD: Now come on, let's hold them walls up.

MARK: *(unbelievably happy for some reason)* Yay! *A B C D!*

DAD: *(amused)* Hurray for the *A B C D*.

(It's possible Mark got excited because of all the spelling of the word "life", which is still not a motto.)

LARRY: How many letters are in the *A B C*?

DAD: *(pretending not to know)* Uh, wait a minute, one, two, three . . . twenty-six.

LARRY: *(immensely proud of himself)* No way! Three! *A, B, C.*

DAD: *(mock-impressed)* Oh ho!

(The tape is stopped and restarted.)

DAD: *(robot voice)* This . . . year . . . several . . . of . . . our . . . children . . . displayed . . . the . . . inherited . . . metaphysical . . . propensity . . . of . . . our . . . line . . .

(Seriously. No shit. This is on the tapes.)

DAD: They . . . asked . . . cosmic . . . questions. On . . . November . . . the . . . twenty-second *(date of JFK'S assassination)*, Larry . . . asked:

LARRY: Is dandruff evil?

DAD: *(mocking Larry's childlike lisp)* Is dangdrugg ebil? *(back to robot voice)* On . . . April . . . the . . . fifteenth *(tax day)*, Danny Doodley-Doo asked:

DANNY: *(lapsing into the Brooklyn accent he picked up from his 2nd grade teacher and has had a hard time shaking ever since)* What happens to your magazine subscriptions after you die?

DAD: Now, we are going to have a whistling exhibition by Mark.

(A beat of silence. Mark gives a small, strangled yelp but is unable to whistle.)

DAD: *(disappointed)* Thank you very much. This is the day that was . . .

DANNY: *(maniacal, singsongy, and clearly jumping his cue)* Good evening, friennnnnnnds!

DAD: Friday . . .

LARRY: March twelfth!

DANNY: Nineteen . . . *(losing his place)* . . . nineteen seventy-six!

DAD: Hurray for Festivus!

MOM: *(tipsy, singing)* "Seventy-six trombones led the big parade . . ."

DANNY: And the walls came tumbling down!

DAD: Oh no, I hope not! We just fixed the roof! Goo-goo-th-th-that's all, folks!

DANNY: *(obsessed with the fucking walls for some reason)* And the walls came tumbling down!

DAD: Look out! *(he makes crashing noises, then whispering)* Crash!

(Danny, Larry, and Mark giggle)

WHAT WE'VE LEARNED FROM THIS ONE

WELL, ALTHOUGH I had not remembered this, there were apparently Festivus speeches and Festivus vows or resolutions declaimed at dinner, which presumably were no more coherent than the rest of this stuff. It makes you wonder how Danny was able to go to school with normal kids, how Larry ended up marrying a woman, and how Mark survived to adulthood.

FESTIVUS 1977
OR "ARE WE DEPRESSED? YES!"

(background noise as people sit down around the tape recorder)

DAD: Now look, don't knock this over.

LARRY: *(snippy)* We won't touch it.

DAD: Aaaaargh!

(it is unclear what "this" was, but it appears safe to say that it was knocked over.)

DAD: —ark wood where the straight—*(stagy Bob Hope voice)* Lemme outta here!

(Part of the tape has been cut off at the beginning, but our father is clearly quoting the first passage in Dante's Inferno, *"In the middle of the journey of our life, I found myself in a dark wood, where the straight way was lost." Apparently, some aspect of our life in the suburbs reminded him of the Florentine's famous vision of hell.)*

DAD: *(pretending to realize where he is)* Oh, hey, whoa. This is a Festivus for the rest of us! Nineteen seventy-seven! The theme of this year is, "We're Not Depressed—Are We?"

DANNY, LARRY, and MARK: *(mumbling)* Yes . . .

DAD: Let's hear it! We're not depressed, are we?

DANNY, LARRY, and MARK: *(yelling)* Yes!!!

DAD: Uh . . . this . . . what kind of a year has it been?

DANNY: Terrible!

MOM: Depressing!

MARK: *(excited)* Yaaaaah!

DAD: We'll never give up, right?

DANNY, LARRY, and MARK: Wrong!

MOM: Oh, we'll give up!

DAD: We've got fortitude and insectitude, right?

*(*Insectitude *is not a word. He may mean by this the indestructible nature of certain insects, such as the cockroach, which are said to be able to survive a nuclear war.)*

DANNY, LARRY, and MARK: Wrong!

DAD: I surrender!

MOM: I give up!

LARRY: We don't got insectitude, we got insecticide!

DAD: This has been—what kind of a year has this been?

MOM: Terrible.

DANNY: Weird!

LARRY: Weird, and terrible!

MARK: Icky! Icky!

DAD: Good evening, this is a Festivus for the Rest of Us. This is March sixteenth, nineteen seventy-seven. The theme of this year is depression. I mean, "We Are Not Depressed!" It has been a very severe winter. People have died. Grandma (my father's mother) died on the nineteenth of January, of a sudden stroke. She was walking to the supermarket, with a friend. She was stricken and leaned over the supermarket cart. And she smiled. She expected it; she was ready for it. She went graciously and quickly. We recovered from that. The winter went on. Other people died. *(deep breath)*

(The tape is stopped and restarted.)

DAD: I am revising my dissertation. I don't know if it's going to work. I am offering it to a publisher as well as to the New School *(for Social Research, the institution that ultimately awarded our father his Ph.D.).* The situation on my job can best be described as . . . insupportable. We are not happy living in Chappaqua, the Indian word for swamp. *(In the Algonquin language.)* Debby suggests that the town might be called "Heritage Swamp." And so you can see why, when I ask, "Are we depressed?" I get this forthright answer: Are we depressed?

DANNY and LARRY: Yes!

DAD: But I believe that everything that rises must converge, and that everything is exactly the same as everything else. And it is these inspiring thoughts that keep us going. Danny, quickly, let's have an inspiring thought, come over here!

DANNY: Then, and here we are talking to you from the Flatiron Building! You're going the right owl pooperman, let's get a word in!

Danny

(It is unclear whether Danny has been instructed to sound incoherent by Dad, or if he is actually just hopped up on sugar.)

DAD: He's got the answer! Disassociation! That's the way to fight depression! Now let's get Larry over here with an idea to fight depression!

LARRY: *(talking, for some reason, like a 1940's radio sports announcer)* Hel-lo, hello sports fans, we're here at the golf meet, and here comes Sluggo with the baseball ba-a-a-at . . . *(he dissolves in giggles)*

DAD: My God, I thought we were in Dayton, Ohio.

(We are not sure what Dayton, Ohio, has to do with anything. However, for information about life, homes, schools, and shopping in the jewel of the Buckeye State, visit: www.dayton-ohio-living.com)

MARK: *(giggling)* Hey, what happened? Hey, why is he using a baseball . . . hat?

MOM: Bat.

MARK: Bat!

DAD: It's the fastest way out of Chappaqua. Anyway. Thank you very much.

(The tape is stopped and restarted.)

DAD: Mark, Mark, give us your . . . help. What have you to say?

MARK: Good evening, friends!

DAD: Thank you very much. Astonishingly, there have been material advances. Enormous increases in salary. Savings accumulating. *(exhales wearily)* But the oxygen . . . is decreasing. Vital bodily functions . . . are diminishing. But we're not depressed, are we?

DANNY, LARRY, and MARK: Yes!

MARK: *(ecstatically)* We are depressed!

DAD: But we shall overcome, won't we?

LARRY: *(dramatically)* Yes, we will!

DAD: You mean life is not like a fountain?

(The tape is stopped and restarted.)

DAD: But we are coping. Danny, under great pressure from the peer group last year, coped and won his way in.

(This is patently untrue.)

DAD: *(cryptically)* Larry is fighting his own battles. *(proudly)* Mark, too shy to go to school at first, is now the hit of the class. Debby, sunk in child rearing, is now *una professoressa* at the *universita di* Vassar.

(This is garbled Italian for "Debby is now a professor at Vassar College.")

DAD: And as for me, *(suddenly shouting)* I'll never give up! I'll never give up! Help, help, let go of me!

(The tape is stopped and restarted.)

DAD: *Allora begorrah, Io ho adesso l'honore de presenterli la granda professoressa.* Deborah, *che vuoi dirle qualche cosa, sul soggetto della esperanza dumano?*

(Okay. We think this might be Italianish for, "now, begorrah, *at this moment I have the honor of presenting the great professor. Deborah, would you like to say something on the subject of human hope?" However, "esperanza" means "hope" in Spanish, not in Italian. And "begorrah" is an Irish nonsense word popular in ethnic jokes.)*

MOM: *(monotone)* Oh no, I've done it again.

DANNY, LARRY, and MARK: Mrs. Jones rides again!

(Note: this refers to the "Mrs. Jones" stories our mom would make up and amuse us with as small children. They always followed this paradigm:

Mrs. Jones is tricked by her small children into leaving the house for some reason. As she leaves, she specifically tells her kids not to do something. Examples of this were burning down the house, painting a neighborhood cat green, and so on. However, it had never occurred to the Jones children to do that particular piece of wickedness. Until their mother mentioned it.

So when Mrs. Jones returns, she finds her demonic brood have done the exact thing she begged them not to. So as they laugh, and the rubble of her house smokes, as a green cat runs around yowling, Mrs. Jones claps her hand to her forehead and ritually intones:

"Oh no, I've done it again!"

Our mother says the inspiration for these stories came from an incident in Louisa May Alcott's Little Men, *where Amy is told not to put beans in her nose. She had never imagined such a thing, but now it is forbidden, and beans in her nose she must have. So she puts beans in her nose, and is in terrible bean-related nasal pain for a good long while.*

   Whatever you may think of these stories, they were incredibly exciting until we were about five.

   Okay, back to 1977.)

MOM: *(clearly being prompted)* What's good this year. *(to our Dad, confused)* What's *good* this year?

DAD: Right, what's good this year?

DANNY, LARRY, and MARK: Nothing's good this year! Three cheers for Mrs. Jones!

MOM: *(sounding mildly annoyed)* Actually, a lot of things are good this year. Our three boys are looking beautiful.

(We most certainly were not.)

Larry

Being very smart, Danny has learned all sorts of things about maps. Larry, complicated math problems. Mark has learned so much in kindergarten that he is the wonder of the classroom, and says sometimes that he wants to be an "adding teacher."

(Presumably, Mark meant a math teacher. He was certainly never gonna be an English teacher at that rate.)

MOM: And once in a while, if I tell them to pick up something, they will even sometimes do it.

DAD: You're right, Mommy, it has been a good year.

We went to Martha's Vineyard. Does anyone remember anything about Martha's Vineyard?

DANNY: I think what was good about Martha's Vineyard was that we got a good place at the Carol Apartments *(a shitty motel)*, and we were very lucky, and it was very good that year. We could do a lot of things; we went to South Beach; we went down to the end of the town *(Fisherman's Wharf)* quite a lot, and we played in the pool.

DAD: Mommy and I went away a few weekends by ourselves.

MOM: That was good.

DAD: That was very good. We went to her reunion at George School, and stayed in New Hope.

Dad, Danny, Larry, and Mark in a headlock.

(George School is the Quaker boarding school in Pennsylvania my mother attended.)

DAD: And we also went to Salisbury, Connecticut. And we're to go away several other weekends this year, including to California. Mommy, you're right, there were good things. There was doing the dissertation, and Mommy wrote an article which she sent out to some magazines.

MOM: Our boys have learned to work hard and are being an enormous help in the yard, having already learned to pick up great bushels of leaves and cart them away, and we're hoping to put them to work and give them more money well earned.

DAD: And tell the various special lessons that they're taking now.

(The tape is stopped and restarted.)

MOM: In the fall, when the weather was good, Danny had an electricity course, in which he learned a lot. Mark had a spectacular gymnastics course, where he jumped on trampolines and did all kinds of things. Larry has been working hard on the piano.

DAD: And tell about their private lessons.

MOM: And Mrs. Stern comes to the house every week and works on interesting math problems and games with Danny and Larry.

DAD: Larry Bunny Rabbit will now let you know what's it like to be seven years old. Tell it like it is, Larry.

LARRY: Well, you see, when you're seven, you have pretty many hardships.

(Swear to God, we talked like that.)

LARRY: *(with growing intensity)* 'Cause mostly when you're seven, you, you usually go to second grade, and second grade is a grade when most people don't really like you very much. But I'm . . . but I'm winning.

(In fact, he was not.)

DAD: Hurray!

LARRY: But it's also very lucky to be seven. And . . . though . . . as . . . but I'm really coming through; I mean it.

DAD: You think you'll make it?

LARRY: Of course I do.

DAD: Every day and every way, better and better?

LARRY: Yup.

DAD: I think you're gonna make it.

LARRY: *(turning on a dime)* Well, I'm not so sure.

MOM: I'd like to ask Larry, what he has been liking to play with most, in the past few months?

LARRY: Legos.

MOM: What do you make with them?

LARRY: *(smugly)* All kinds of things.

DAD: *(sinister German accent)* In fekt, dere is zome sings he is making vich iss highly classified.

(The tape is stopped and restarted.)

DAD: Mommy was talking about yard work and outside. Now let's talk about inside. Danny, how does it feel inside? Inside you?

DANNY: *(unconvincingly)* It feels . . . relatively good.

DAD: It does feel good? I told you he was tough.

DANNY: Well, pretty good. Not many people like me, but I don't care so much.

DAD: *(dramatically)* Why don't people like us? What's wrong with us?

DANNY: *(growing agitated)* I'll tell you why people don't like me. 'Cause I used to have the disgusting habit of picking my nose and rubbing it on my knee, but now I don't anymore, and people . . . and people somehow . . . ah, think that I still do it. I think they should see a psychiatrist.

DAD: I never heard of his rubbing it on his knee, I thought it was—

MOM: It was his elbow.

DAD: I thought it was on his sweater.

DANNY: I didn't wear sweaters then. In second grade I refused to wear sweaters.

(Mom and Dad laugh heartily at this.)

DAD: So would I! So would I! Are we depressed?

MOM: *(giggling)* Yes!

DANNY, LARRY, and MARK: Yes!

DAD: *(effeminate, upper-crust British accent)* Danny, I strongly suspect that you have this, um . . . great quality of being tough, that you're egosyntonic.

(e•go-syn•ton•ic Pronunciation: [ī′gȳ-sin-ton′ik, eg′ȳ-]),
—adj. Psychiatry.
of or pertaining to aspects of one's behavior or attitudes viewed as acceptable and consistent with one's fundamental personality and beliefs (contrasted with ego-dystonic).
—RANDOM HOUSE UNABRIDGED DICTIONARY

(Uhhh . . . thanks, Dad? I think?)

DAD: Umm, you stand up to it alright. You don't let it get you down, is that right?

(Danny doesn't answer, and Mom and Dad start pretending to bawl like a baby, making fun of him.)

DANNY: *(angrily)* I'm not so sure!

DAD: Get up, Danny, get up. Stop crying! Help him, quickly, help him!

(The tape is stopped and restarted.)

Mark

DAD: One half hour later, Danny has recovered consciousness. Alright, Danny, how do you feel now?

(Silence.)

DANNY: *(barely audible)* Okay.

DAD: Alright, now I'd like to ask Mark some questions. I want to ask Mark how it feels *outside*. Namely, outside you. How does it feel to be outside you, looking at all those other people, enjoying you?

(As far as we remember, this is just philosophical babble and does not refer to some sort of group sexual assault.)

MARK: I would like it better if I was, if I was inside out.

(Hey, maybe it does.)

DAD: But Mark, your inside *is* out. You are outgoing to the inside of the other outsiders, right?

MARK: *(giggling with delight)* No!

DAD: Are we depressed?

DANNY, LARRY, and MARK: Yes!

MOM: *(depressed, moaning sound)* Ohhhhhh.

DANNY: But we will make it!

DAD: But depression is good for you, right?

DANNY, LARRY, and MARK: No!

DAD: I knew it was bad. *(BBC announcer's English accent)* Good evening, ladies and gentlemen. We're now talking to a psychological marvel here. We have in our studio a young boy *(his English accent abruptly veers from plummy to Cockney)* who was unable to go to school without a bag on his head.

(This is absolutely true. Mark was very shy in nursery school, and for a while, wouldn't go unless he could wear a paper bag over his head, with eyeholes my mom cut for him.)

DAD: *(his English accent becomes fancy once again)* But he was so successful in this that now all the children his age wear bags on their heads, absolutely all the time. *(in a Dean Martin-like drunk-guy voice)* There is a rule in nursery school, absolutely no one is admitted without a bag on his head.

(Children giggle in the background.)

DAD: But seriously, we have here a little boy who was shy when he started school, and now isn't shy and has lots of friends. Mark, why are you enjoying kinder-garten so much? *(whispers)* Be serious.

MARK: I dunno.

DAD: But you're happy there, aren't you?

MARK: Yeah.

DAD: You have friends?

MARK: No.

DAD: You don't need friends, do you? Do we need friends?

DAD, DANNY, LARRY, and MARK: No!

DAD: Mark, you're always so happy at school. Why do you like it so much?

MARK: *(genuinely puzzled)* I don't know! Maybe because the teacher's so nice.

DAD: I think the teacher likes you. Who's your teacher?

MARK: Mrs. Bernstein.

DAD: Judy Bernstein? Oh, Judy liked Larry very much. You know, Mrs. Bernstein sent a note home. What did the note about Mark say?

MOM: It said "Mark is just terrific, and I like having him in my class so much."

DAD: Did you know that?

MARK: Yes. I remember a lotta stuff.

DAD: What else do you remember?

MARK: When . . . you were using that tape recorder lasht weer . . . when, when it was Festivus.

DAD: Aha.

MARK: And Dad, where's my dollar for re-amembering that?

DAD: That's right, we had a contest to see . . .

DANNY: Why don't I get a dollar?

DAD: . . .who could remember things last Festivus, and Mark won. This is the nineteen seventy-seven Festivus, the fifteenth annual celebration of you-know-what!

(Dad, Danny, and Larry cackle with staged, maniacal laughter.)

MOM: Hey, who invited them?

(The tape is stopped and restarted.)

DAD: It's nature, it's nature. We were all so stressed and busy that Mommy did everything for this Festivus all by herself. *(answering himself in an Edward G. Robinson impression)* Hey, wait a minute, she always did! Didn't she? *(regular voice)* I would like to ask Mommy, who was the author of this feast, what we did, what we had at Festivus, this fifteenth anniversary of you-know-what.

MOM: At Festivus dinner this year, each boy made a story or a picture about the family, that were very attractive and interesting.

(The rest of the 1977 recording is lost.)

WHAT WE'VE LEARNED FROM THIS ONE

JUST HOW MUCH of these recordings were staged comedy bits interspersed with the serious questions, reminiscences, and unstaged silliness. None of us remembered that sometimes at Festivus dinner, each one of us told a story he'd written, or showed a picture he'd drawn about the family or someone in the family. Also, "Heritage Swamp" is definitely a better name for the town than "Chappaqua."

OTHER ODD FAMILY HOLIDAYS AND RITUALS

UNBIRTHDAYS:

Named of course after the holiday in Lewis Carroll's *Alice in Wonderland*, a frenzied feast celebrated by animals and lunatics. Similarly, in our house these were birthday-like celebrations that had nothing to do with anyone's actual birthday. Theoretically, they were birthday parties held by our parents in the honor of a specific child, to cheer him up after something unfortunate occurred at school or home. The promise of an Unbirthday was a quick and cheap emotional Band-Aid to an upset kid, used in the same way the management of a dangerous carnival might give out free passes to dazed customers injured on the rides.

THE POLISH HOUR

The Polish Hour was a sort of live action radio show that sometimes took place after dinner, by the ebbing candlelight of dinner. Once a year or so, we would assume the Polish Hour position: Dad would sit by the dining room window in an ancient, yellow, frayed armchair; Mom would sit at the piano; and us kids would be strewn about. Mom would play a piano exercise called "Polish Dances" from one of Larry's old piano instruction books. Then Dad would begin his one-man radio show with the words "This is the Polish Hour." His monologue largely concerned itself with "Life in the Swamp," which was what he called our town, Chappaqua, as previously noted. Dad would yarn amusingly about our lives in the past tense, as if describing the doings of a peculiar Depression-era town, where fantastical things happened. Topics in this monologue included bizarre and fantastical sufferings and injustices we had apparently endured, as well as the tremendous amount of rain that took place in "the Swamp." This lasted for up to an hour.

FAMILY ELECTIONS

Our father frequently announced that free and fair elections would soon take place in our household. However, he had imperfectly learned the principles of democracy, for the Family Presidential Elections usually consisted of Dad, at family dinner, arbitrarily appointing middle brother Larry to be president. We remember that Mark was occasionally appointed vice president, or secretary. Needless to say, this created great animosity among the brothers. After dinner, the government usually got its ass kicked.

HAVE A SIP OF WINE, MAKE A FUNNY FACE

This was done when we were very young. Mom or Dad at dinner would say, "Have a sip of wine, make a funny face," and we would wrap our tiny hands around his or her wineglass, take a small swallow, and invariably screw up our faces in a child's disgust at the bitter taste of alcohol. This ended abruptly when Mom thought it would be cute to do this at a dinner party, but Danny got stage fright, bit when he should have sipped, and chomped a mouth-shaped piece out of her wineglass, much to the horror of the assembled guests. Fortunately, he didn't swallow it, or he would've had his own page that year in the elementary school yearbook.

FESTIVUS 1980

OR: "TOO EASILY MADE GLAD?"

DAD: *(hillbilly accent)* I'm busted, disgusted, and I cain't be trusted. *(his accent has now become that of an elderly bluesman)* We busted one machine trying to make this here Festivus, get this here Festivus on the road.

(Earlier that week, we had tried to make a Festivus recording, but the ancient Dictaphone finally gave out. Also, the "busted and disgusted" line is one Dad heard from a couple of Kentucky girls in high school, which made a great impression on him—he repeats it to this day.)

DAD: This is a Festivus for the rest of us. This is the year of the wimp and Donald Duck.

(The wimp refers to beloved humanitarian and former President Jimmy Carter, whom our dad was not fond of. He called him that because of a small scandal that year at the Boston Globe *newspaper: an editor had entitled a speech by Carter "More Mush from the Wimp." Donald Duck may refer to Ronald Reagan.)*

DAD: *Ducko wimpeque consule.*

(In half-assed Latin, this probably means, "the duck and the wimp are consuls." Which was a high Roman government official.)

DAD: And things are bad in the country, but things are good in the family. This is May third, nineteen eighty. Danny is eleven, Mark is eight, Larry is ten, Mommy is forty, and I am one hundred and fifty-two years old. Last year our motto was *Coraggio!*. . .

(In three-quarter-assed Italian, this probably means "courage!")

DAD: . . . and "Don't Give Up the Ship!" and "Overcome Fellacity." Now, this year . . .

(Dad clearly loses his train of thought. The tape is stopped and restarted.)

DAD: And this year our motto is . . .

LARRY: "What Happen Next?"

(That was one of Larry's first and favorite sentences when he was a baby. Probably because all of us rarely had any idea what would happen next, at any given time.)

DAD: Or as Mommy puts it . . .

MOM: Can We Top This?

DAD: Or as Danny says it . . .

DANNY: Are We Pushovers?

DAD: Or as I say, Too Easily Made Glad? We're doing better . . . in some ways. Danny published two poems . . .

(In a children's literary magazine called Stone Soup. *It was not reviewed by any major media outlets, and the movie rights remain unbought.)*

DAD: . . . and then Mommy published in the *New York Times* and *American Heritage* . . .

(The American Heritage *piece was a historical interest piece about my mother's grandmother, but the* Times *article was a humor piece about poorly written real estate ads she'd found, advertising house features like a: "huge elk!" Because of misprinting an* l *for an* i, *an eat-in kitchen was being sold as a large, northern deer possessing enormous, flattened antlers in the male. Another house boasted of a "westerly sunset.")*

DAD: . . . and was encouraged by the *New Yorker,* and then I sold my book to Seabury Press as a Continuum Book, it'll be published next year—Danny don't pick your nose—um, for about a hundred and fifty dollars, about five hundred copies, of which four hundred will be remaindered. I'm doing better at work; I'm in charge of their Mickey-Mouse paperback books, and various line assignments and getting the originals in, and going to California again, and it's clearer, more than ever, what a (unintelligible) job it is. And the big thing is that we bought a house. Mark, tell us where the house is.

MARK: Our house is in Ripton, Vermont.

DAD: Where in Ripton, Vermont? It's on Middle— it's on Breadloaf Mountain, near Middlebury *(yawns)* College. How often have we gone up there already?

MARK: Twelve times.

DAD: We go up on weekends. So far, what kinds of things have happened to us on the way?

LARRY: Well, once we broke down after Mom was singing *(sings like a frog)* "Moving right along . . ."

(From The Muppet Movie. *And the two thoughts are*

*unrelated: the car breaking down was unrelated to
our mother's singing.)*

DANNY: Once we had a power blackout, and we bundled Mark in sheets.

DAD: Once, there was a break-in, and another time, the pipes burst.

(The tape is stopped and restarted.)

DAD: The family had an interesting summer. The boys went to a baseball camp. We planted twelve new gardens in the back and had picnics back there. We put eight new window boxes on the house. We fixed the grill and started charcoaling on the terrace. And we got our Chappaqua house fixed up real nice. The house in Ripton is near cross-country ski trails. Unfortunately it was very hot during the winter, and we weren't able to do any skiing. And unfortunately we're too busy this summer for Mommy to go to the Bread Loaf Conference or for me to go to the German school . . .

(The Bread Loaf Writers Conference is an annual writers' retreat near Ripton, Vermont, where our mother took classes. The German school was the summer German program offered by Middlebury College, which is known for the quality of its language programs, and the prodigious marijuana intake of its students.)

DAD: That's something we may do in the future.

(Bread Loaf and German, not marijuana.)

DAD: Just a few other highlights: the boys all got new bikes and went to baseball camp. They formed their own rock group.

(Actually our dad formed it, and managed it like a slightly more intense Joe Jackson from the Jackson Five. The group had no name and no instruments, but under our father's direction, the three of us sang Billy Joel, Willie Nelson, and Barry Manilow songs in the barns, garages, and living rooms of our relatives, who listened out of a mixture of politeness and curiosity.)

DAD: I will ask each of them some of the things that they have done. Danny, tell me some of the things you did this year.

DANNY: This year I got into Mrs. Scott's sixth grade, and I have a teacher who is trying to *(screaming)* Get me!

DAD: What about your poetry contest?

DANNY: Oh, and I also won a poetry contest. It's on a white *(mispronouncing the word* plaque*)* plague, which is now hanging in Mrs. Fritschler's room. And she will give it back to us after a while.

DAD: This was a countywide contest. The poems were circulated through the Westchester library and appeared in the Congressional Record . . .

(There is the sound of a beer being opened)

DAD: . . . and Danny got a letter from his congressman about it. Danny, I would like you to read one of the Eskimo poems now.

DANNY: Both?

DAD: Go ahead.

(Note to reader: You must be out of your damn mind

if you think I'd reprint some horrible crap I wrote
when I was eleven.)

DAD: Larry, what kind of a year has it been for you?

LARRY: Well, over last summer, I went to this rotten
baseball camp. The coaches were very mean to everyone, whether they were good, good players or not.
Also, this spring, I am in a baseball league for Westchester. I mean, um, New Castle Recreation Depart-
ment, and I won our first game with a walk. Um, I had
a perfect report card the last time we had it, except for
a bad mark in organization. *(He whistles for no apparent
reason.)* Um, I'm doing very well in piano, and I always
take violin. I am, I was in, in the All-County Music
Festival as a second violin. Um, my mom and dad and
everyone thinks that the orchestra part was one of the
best. Also, our class, Mr. Brownsword's class, is doing
the play by Gilbert and Sullivan, *The Pirates of Pen-
zance.* I am the Major-General in it.

DAD: Sing it!

LARRY: And now, I will sing for you the song, "I Am
the Very Model of a Modern Major-General."

*"I am the very model of a modern Major-General,
I've information vegetable, animal, and mineral,
I know the kings of England, and I quote the fights historical
From Marathon to Waterloo, in order categorical;
I'm very well acquainted, too, with matters mathematical,
I understand equations, both the simple and quadratical,
About binomial theorem I'm teeming with a lot o' news,
With many cheerful facts about the square of the
hypotenuse."*

DAD: And now Mark; what kind of a year has it been?

MARK: It's been pretty good, because I have gone to Washington to visit my relatives, and I've gone to Hillside where the food is terrible and a lotta kids—

DAD: That's camping out, for two days, right, Mark?

MARK: —yeah, and a lotta kids threw up.

DAD: And they made you move to a special room—

MARK: Jim threw up, too.

DAD: —because you talked about throwing up so much, isn't that right, Mark?

MARK: They said I was talking about sick things, like food, and *(voice rising)* I wasn't! I mean all I— after Peter Lizer threw up—I just was talking about how yucky it tastes after you throw up.

DAD: And they made you go sleep with the teacher, right, Mark?

MARK: Yeah, they did.

MOM: *(alarmed)* What?

DAD: Was that yucky?

MARK: Yeah, that was yucky, really yucky.

DAD: Okay, what else happened this year you liked?

MARK: *(proudly)* I threw up.

DAD: *(cracking up)* Yeah, no, I mean, like about like your bike, you got a new bike.

MARK: I got a new bike.

DAD: How didja get the bike, Mark?

MARK: I earned it, and I got walkie-talkies, with built-in radio.

(These never worked. Not once.)

MARK: And, um, I'm gonna burp.

DAD: And how did you earn all this money?

MARK: I raked leaves. *(he burps loudly)* Blaaaah!

DAD: You were a very good raker. And what else happened during the year?

MARK: Well, *(thinks seriously)* I threw up.

DAD: Yes, well, I remember something that happened. You and Mommy and the other boys learned how to read several of Shakespeare's plays aloud, and you became such good readers that up in Vermont, in the Robert Frost country where our house is, you read to an astonished Granny a Robert Frost poem about the day the bones went up the stairs.

(This refers to a Robert Frost poem called "The Witch of Coös." It describes a skeleton buried in a couple's cellar that wakes up and starts coming topside, annoyed that it had been murdered by the husband in a fight over the wife. The husband kills it again. It's like a New England Gothic version of Desperate Housewives.*)*

DAD: Would you read a few lines from that now, if Mommy can find it?

MARK: Yeah, if *(incomprehensible mumbling)*.

(We hear a book being opened.)

MOM: Start where it says, "And then someone . . ."

DAD: Go ahead and read, Mark.

MARK:

"And then someone
Began the stairs, two footsteps for each step,
The way a man with one leg and a crutch,
Or a little child, comes up. It wasn't Toffile:
It wasn't anyone who could be there.
The bulkhead double-doors were double-locked
And swollen tight and buried under snow.
The cellar windows were banked up with sawdust
And swollen tight and buried under snow.
It was the bones. I knew them—and good reason.
My first impulse was to get to the knob
And hold the door. But the bones didn't try
The door; they halted helpless on the landing,
Waiting for things to happen in their favor.
The faintest restless rustling ran all through them.
I never could have done the thing I did
If the wish hadn't been too strong in me
To see how they were mounted for this walk.
I had a vision of them put together
Not like a man, but like a chandelier.
So suddenly I flung the door wide on him.
A moment he stood balancing with emotion,
And all but lost himself. (A tongue of fire
Flashed out and licked along his upper teeth.
Smoke rolled inside the sockets of his eyes.)
Then he came at me with one hand outstretched,
The way he did in life once; but this time
I struck the hand off brittle on the floor,
And fell back from him on the floor myself.

The finger-pieces slid in all directions.
(Where did I see one of those pieces lately?
Hand me my button-box—it must be there.)"

DAD: And so the bones went up the stairs, clickety-clack, and Mark made Granny's hair stand on end.

(Note: in our family, it is considered polite to drive an elderly woman to a remote, rural area, and tell her ghost stories that involve skeletons coming for you.)

DAD: And what kind of a Festivus has it been? It has been a wonderful Festivus. As usual, we had the traditional turkey and Champagne, and Festivus poems and songs, and gradually the mystery of Festivus . . . is being revealed. And to the young initiates, during the course of the next year, we will reveal the suitable passages in the ancient rites, in the old rite . . .

MARK: *(hacking cough)*

DAD: . . . that are appropriate to what Festivus attempts to bring about. Festivus is a mystery, and a resurrection, and now, Mommy, what kind of a year has it been?

MOM: It's been a very complicated year, and things seem to be looking up. I went from Vassar to being unemployed, getting unemployment insurance.

DAD: That was good.

MOM: Starting in, to try some magazine writing, not knowing where it would go, but I have managed to sell a short piece to *American Heritage*, and pieces to the *New York Times* Westchester section, and I have taught half-time at Manhattan College, which was a revelation to me. I may get a job at Manhattanville or somewhere else for next year, or I may stay home and write marvelous, unprecedented things.

Castle von Festivus

DAD: And now, I would like to ask Mommy to read from a still-unpublished article, the first that she wrote. The one that Roger Angell of the *New Yorker* so liked. Just the beginning of a poem *(clears throat)* I, uh, not a poem, a piece which I always think of as being about being back in the kitchen again, but Mommy has a different title. Go ahead.

MOM: The title is "So It Wasn't a Total Loss." (FYI—the title "So It Wasn't a Total Loss" is taken from a student evaluation of my mother's teaching, from when she was a professor at Vassar College. This jackass said that he hated my mom's class and found it near-useless, except that the papers she assigned provided him with typing practice . . . "so it wasn't a total loss." What an asshole. Pray I never find you, punk.) These are the first sentences:

"The layer of grease in last night's frying pan is smooth and opaque. I stare at the tiny mouseprints crossing it and going nowhere. They make me think of our endless parade of rodents: the mouse who once watched television with the children, the mouse under the radiator, the mouse with its droppings in my closet. I do not want to think yet about the incident of the mouse and the oven. I also don't want to think about my fortieth birthday last week, or about my lost job."

(The tape is stopped and restarted.)

DAD: This is the nineteenth annuavershary. The nineteenth annual . . . ahh . . . the nineteenth annual Festivus. The eighteenth anniversary of the mystery of the bag and the clock, *und so weider, und so weider.*

(German for "and so on.")

DAD: And here we are, and the theme of this Festivus is . . .

LARRY: *(Muppet voice)* What! Happen! Next!

DANNY: And . . . *(remembering)* Are We Pushovers?

MOM: *(sounding exhausted)* Can We Top This?

DAD: Or in other words, are we Too Easily Made Glad? *(Our father now starts to talk in some kind of jivey beatnik accent)* Just because we saw a little dark at the end of the tunnel, just because we got a little "An Der Freude," 'cause we got a little "Coraggio," just because we—the ship didn't go down, at least under the last wave, ah, are we Too Easily Made Glad? Um, I think we *are* too easily made glad; we've had some mild success this year, *(disgustedly)* and we bask in it. *(sighs)* But all it should do is to remind us of our talents and of our responsibilities, which we squander . . . *(despondently)* here in the swamp.

(The tape is stopped and restarted)

DAD: *(chuckling)* Isn't that a cheerful mood?

MOM: Whoop de doo!

DAD: We have a few Festivus poems, starting with the mommy!

MOM: Starting with Danny.

DAD: No, starting with Danny, a Festivus poem!

DANNY:
"Festivus 1980"
(Clearly written by Dad.)
"Well, we can look back on this year and call it shit,
But we're none the worse for it.
As some immortal poet said,
At least we don't have bugs in bed.
So thank your lucky stars
That none of us spends time in bars.
Festivus Eighty comes and goes,
And we sit and drool and count our toes,
So when Dad opens a beer,
Open up with a rousing cheer,
Because we're lucky to have each other.
So hug your brother and hug your mother,
But be careful not to step on her toes,
Or she'll punch you in the nose.
And don't believe that Dad's a bore,
For his piles of moldy lore

Aren't meant to get you sore,
And are brightened by an occasional roar.
At every ring of the phone,
Mom tends to mourn and groan.
She's strange and she's odd,
But to us she's God,
As she screams to an empty dial tone."

DAD: Now, Mark, what do you think?

MARK: *(troubled)* I don't know.

DAD: What do you mean you don't know? Bright kid like you don't know? Send him back to school.

(The tape is stopped and restarted)

DAD: Are we too easily made glad? Here's Mommy's poem.

MOM: I have three poems, about three people, and when I have read them I would like you all to say who the person is. The first:

"He races, he jumps, and he bikes.
He outruns us all on our hikes.
He goes off on long trips
And he roars and he skips,
And he does just whatever he likes."

LARRY AND DANNY: Mark! Mark!

DAD: Marco Polar Bear! Hurray for the Bobo! Next!

MOM: (clears throat)
"When an adult commands him or preaches,
He generally grumbles and screeches.
But he's funny and cool

And the top of the school,
And he's talked of in Congress' speeches."

DAD: Hurray for Danny Doodleydoo!

MOM: Yay, Danny!

MOM:
"He won't eat his tuna or yolks
But his fiddling brings joy to all folks.
He won't tie his sneaks
But whenever he speaks
He delights us with wisdom and jokes."

LARRY: That's me!

DAD: Larry Bunnyrabbit!. Now I've got—I'm having a little interview here. Oh look, I've found a little rabbit!

LARRY: *(weird, quavery voice)* He-e-e-elp!

DAD: Oh rabbit, don't be frightened.

LARRY: He-e-e-elp!

DAD: We're going to take you home!

LARRY: He-e-e-elp!

DAD: We like rabbits at our house!

LARRY: He-e-e-elp!

DAD: We're actually queer for rabbits!

LARRY: *(kicking it up a notch)* He-e-e-elp!

(This stylized, ritual rape threat/comedy bit was occasionally repeated on long car rides, and in front of company. Our family, while well-disposed toward rabbits, is not

actually queer for them. We are, however, queer for squir-
rels, chipmunks, chickens, raccoons, and the huge, filthy,
South American rodent known as the capybara.)

DAD: Last year at Festivus, a rare treat. Danny had a
little group. And they sang some very current songs
like, "In the Navy," "Lola". . .

(Note: not the Kinks' song about the drag queen, he means
Barry Manilow's "Copacabana," about Lola the showgirl
and Tony the bartender.)

DAD: Things like that, that I hadn't heard. He went on
to do it in our weekend at *(Aunt)* Eileen's, on Eileen's
stage *(in a shed)*, then again for *(cousin)* Martha in the
summer, and then at a little Christmas party for
Granny. The group is a little inactive now; they're
learning some new stuff, some Pink Floyd, but here's a
retrospect on last year's performances . . . Danny!

(Here follows a rendition of "Copacabana" as performed
by three preteen boys. Yup, it's hot.)

(The tape is stopped and restarted.)

DANNY: *(cause of pain unclear)* Oww! Oww!

DAD: In memoriam to the departed, to Grandma
O'Keefe, who left us now a little over three years ago.
To *(Uncle)* Charlie, who left before that. And then to
the living dead also, to *(name witheld)*, who joined the
Loonies, I do mean the Moonies.

(An unidentified child is heard, quietly sobbing in the back-
ground.)

DAD: And to all the people who are not as happy as we

are, I want to say one thing. We weren't always happy either, and we've learned that it . . . takes hard work, and that it is a form, even, of "coraggio." Right? Are we pushovers, are we too easily made glad, what happens next, and can you top this? Mommy, your thoughts.

MOM: My thoughts are, we've been doing a lot of things, and we're going to be doing more—Mark! Have you seen any movies!

MARK: Yeah.

MOM: What movies have you seen?

MARK: *Escape to Witch Mountain* at . . . at Hillside where they serve terrible food—

MOM: *(tries to shut him down)* O-kay . . .

MARK: —and a couple of kids threw up—

MOM: Mark! What . . . what movies have you all seen together? Larry?

LARRY: Well, we saw *Grease* a while ago.

MOM: That's right.

LARRY: And we saw the *Black Stallion* very *(searches for a word)* uh, um, soon, a long . . . recently!

DAD: You saw *Grease*, I saw "Sweat."

(Mom laughs.)

LARRY: And we're hoping—

MOM: I saw "Tears"! "Blood"!

LARRY: And we're hoping to see, um, *The Empire Strikes Back.*

DAD: I saw "Saliva."

DANNY: *(authoritatively)* The sequel to *Star Wars.*

MOM: Not to mention "Excrement"!

(Original title of You've Got Mail.*)*

MOM: "Excrement," I saw in the backyard. Danny, what else is in our backyard?

DANNY: Bones of little animals.

MOM: That's right.

(This is true. There were animal bones all over the backyard. It could have been where neighborhood cats would abandon their half-eaten prey, it could be the result of one of us hitting moles with the mower, or maybe our neighbors practiced voodoo. But it was creepy as hell.)

DANNY: Rolls of toilet paper. Discarded, mashed toys, and to top it off, *(suddenly hysterical with laughter)* glazed bagels!

(If this was slang for something, nobody remembers what it meant.)

MOM: Alright, what did we all read this winter, together? *King . . .*

DANNY, LARRY, and MARK: *Lear!*

MOM: This Festivus is dedicated to King Lear and his amazing daughters in hopes that . . . our sons will remember . . . to . . .

(Mom and Dad dissolve in laughter.)

DAD: Alright, we gotta get a better dedication than

that. I gotta take this over. Listen now, last year what pulled us through was our dedication. We were down in the dumps, Daddy was just about totally smashed, and we dedicated it to "coraggio," right, we dedicated it to overcoming fellacity, and we dedicated it to . .

(He begins to hum the Ode To Joy. *Lyrics by Frederich Schiller, music from Beethoven's* Ninth Symphony, fourth movement. *The rest of the family joins in the humming)*

DAD: No, no, with words.

DANNY, LARRY, and MARK: *Freude, schöner Götterfunken,*

DAD: That was good.

DANNY, LARRY, and MARK: *Tochter aus Elysium,*

DAD: You better believe it!

DANNY, LARRY, and MARK: *Wir betreten feuertrunken,*

DAD: Every day and every way!

DANNY, LARRY, and MARK: *Himmlische, dein Heiligtum!*

DAD: It's good for ya, too!

DANNY, LARRY, and MARK: *Deine Zauber binden wieder,*

DAD: Have a little every day.

DANNY, LARRY, and MARK: *Was die Mode streng geteilt: alle Menschen werden Brüder,*

DAD: It pulled us through the year.

DANNY, LARRY and MARK:

Wo dein snafter Flügel weilt.
(English translation:
"Joy, beautiful spark of the gods,
Daughter of Elysium,
We enter fire imbibed,
Heavenly, thy sanctuary.
Thy magic reunites those
Whom stern custom has parted;
All men will become brothers
Under thy gentle wing.)

MOM: To Freud!

DAD: No, To Joy, to Joy.

MARK: Pink Floyd!

DAD: No listen, we're going on this next year, we
are . . . going to be greedy. That is the motto for next
year. Greed!

(Hey, it was 1980.)

DAD: We made it so far, we made it so far by joy, and
now we're too easily made glad. *(coughs)* We're
pushovers! Daddy gets a lousy twelve thousand dollar
raise, and we all cheer. Cheer!

DANNY, LARRY, and MARK: Yay! Woo!

DAD: Mommy publishes a lousy couple of—*(she giggles)* I mean, an excellent four or five articles, and
everybody cheers. Cheer!

ALL: Yay!

DAD: Danny publishes some poetry, it gets in the

Congressional Record, and we're pushovers. *(coughs almost to the point of vomiting)* Cheer!

DANNY, LARRY, and MOM: *(slightly concerned)* Yay . . .

MARK: Rah! Rah! Rah!

DAD: I tell you, we've got to set our heights higher, and so the motto for next year is "Greed!" Let's hear it for greed!

DANNY, LARRY, and MARK: Yay, greed!

DANNY: Mine! Mine!

MOM: Mine! Mine!

DAD: Alright, we'll see you next year *(ominous)* and see how far "Greed!" got us . . . good-bye!

WHAT WE'VE LEARNED FROM THIS ONE

MARK WAS JUST as obsessed with vomit then as he is now.

FESTIVUS 1985

(no theme)

DAD: Testing for Festing, testing for Festing.

(We hear forty-five seconds of nothing but a scratchy LP record playing; it is of creepy, atonal classical music that sounds like the soundtrack to a Hitchcock film. We can't identify it.)

DAD: This is . . . Festivus.

(More creepy music.)

DAD: This could be . . . the last Festivus. I hope not.

(More music, heavy on the oboe.)

DAD: This is a Festivus . . . for the rest of us. November twenty-eighth, nineteen eighty-five. We are minus one.

(The tape is stopped and restarted.)

DAD: And so this is a Festivus for what's left of us. On June eighth, nineteen eighty-five, Granny, Harriet Crawford *(Mom's mother)*, Granny, after a long illness, died. Debby, tell us how it happened.

MOM: Granny had a terrible time at the last part of her illness. When she couldn't eat at all, she had to choose whether to have a complicated and dreadful operation, and she decided because it was the only hopeful thing left, she would do it. It didn't work, and she died a couple of weeks later, after having a lot of discouragement and pain.

But at the same time, she had done a very brave and tough and humorous job of keeping going. I remember coming into her room in the nursing center, uh, maybe ten days before she died, and finding her sitting up, entertaining several old friends, and acting like a hostess and *grande dame* as she always did. We'll think about the two and a third years that she was very sick, and all the fun that we had in those times, the times that we all went over to Thirty-Thirty *(a retirement community in Bridgeport, Connecticut)* and had parties and occasions. And it was a time we wouldn't want to be without, so we are grateful to her for those New Years and Christmases and Thanksgivings and all kinds of occasions, and remember how brave she was, but also how much fun we had, during this whole complicated and mostly dreadful period.

(The tape is stopped and restarted.)

DAD: Our Festivuses have been happening all of a year and a half apart. So just two back, and Mark's in grade school. You have to go two back for the first sign of Granny's illness. And she carried it so well that when you go one back, a year and a half ago, we weren't even mentioning it. Because she was standing up, and let's say the word, though we didn't at the time, cancer. She did a beautiful job, and we had a memorial service for her in Saint Francis Church on Long Ridge Road in Stamford *(Connecticut)*, where Debby and I had been married, twenty-one years earlier. It was the first time we went back. And I was asked, along with *(Uncle)* Mark Ball, to do a eulogy. Mark's not here at the moment, but here's what I said. On June fourteenth *(clears throat)*, nineteen eighty-five.

There follows a very moving rendition of the actual eulogy for our grandmother, Harriet Crawford Janney. It mentions her decades of social work, placing thousands of children for adoption, her strong Christian values, and her love for her family. It doesn't seem appropriate to print it in a book designed to separate bored business travelers in airports from their money, when they're out of thrillers set in the Vatican.

(The tape is stopped and restarted, and then we hear the opening piano chords of Billy Joel's New York State of Mind.*)*

DANNY: *(muffled)* We created a monster.

DAD: Shh.

LARRY: Are we on yet? *(in an exaggerated stoner voice)* Whoops . . . hey . . . what? This, this is a Festivus for . . . us. And what kind of a year has it been, man? *(to Danny)* Yo, fool, I'm asking you, man. *(Danny flips him off)* Oh, you can't say that on the radio, man. Okay. Well, this is where we are. We're in Thanksgiving, and Vermont. And Dan is seventeen, and I'm sixteen, and Mark is fourteen. That means—

MOM: Tomorrow.

LARRY: What?

MOM: Tomorrow.

LARRY: Aw, Jesus, tomorrow is Mark's birthday, and this is Thanksgiving Day on . . . November twenty-seventh. Dad was wrong. And tomorrow's the twenty-eighth. Dan's a senior. I am a junior, and Mark is starting his first year in high school as a freshman. May I repeat, Mark is a freshman.

MARK: *(giggling)* A studly freshman.

LARRY: I . . . I . . . I don't think so. You're, you're just a freshman, Mark. This is the first Festivus we've had since before the Europe trip, and, well, we took off to Europe and spent thirty-three days there. It was England, France, and, uh, Amsterdam and Germany, and Vienna, places like that.

(He's leaving out Venice, Florence, Barcelona, Madrid, and Lisbon. We covered a hell of a lot of ground in a month.)

LARRY: And we have some unbiased opinions on that, coming first from our resident freshman. Mark O'Keefe. And do you think you can handle this, Mark?

MARK: *(annoyed silence)*

LARRY: Well, Mark's a freshman. So I'll let Dad do it. Go for it, Dad.

DAD: *(in German) In Deutschland haben wir neu—*

LARRY: *(disgustedly)* Ah, come on, Dad, give it up.

DAD: Okay! We went and we talked the language of every country when we were in the country. On the

Champs Elysee, where we were sitting for light aperitifs immediately after the Tour de France, I had my second full bottle of wine for the day.

DANNY: *(amused)* Hah!

DAD: There were a couple of long-nosed French couples sitting next to us, *(Mark cracks up)* and I was giving a rather long speech on France, and I remember that I said—

DANNY: *"Dos muchachos!"*

(Danny is quoting Dad's refrain throughout the trip. It was "Dos muchachos despues de me!" Meaning "two boys behind me!"

It referred to the formation we were supposed to walk in on foreign sidewalks, like so:

MARK

MOM   **DAD**

LARRY   **DANNY**

The idea was that his two older sons would act as a screen against pickpockets and robbers. He had become paranoid when two Spaniards attempted to rob him, and so apparently was willing to sacrifice Danny and Larry to the knives of bandits attacking from behind, and Mark to a frontal assault.

This was not popular among us.

(Dad now goes into a long, rambling speech in French that we can't decipher except for "vive la France!")

LARRY and MARK: *(heckle him)*

DANNY: You are humiliating yourself!

(Dad promptly switches to a long, rambling speech in German that is entirely incomprehensible.)

LARRY: Dad. Dad!

DAD: When we were in Portugal, I would do things like check into the hotel in English—

LARRY: With your fly open.

DAD: —and then explain in bad Portuguese to the kids, and they didn't know who we were, and when we came home, there was a sort of a turning point in the life of this family. I was deposed, just as my father was deposed before me. Danny brought the boys, the pookers as I used to call them, together, they formed a thin rank—

MARK: *(belches loudly)*

DAD: —and they said, "Daddy, we don't ever want to do that again."

(The tape is stopped and restarted.)

LARRY: *(stuck in the damn stoner voice)* This Festivus is a hotbed of turgid emotions here.

DANNY: Turgid?

LARRY: Turgid.

DAD: This is Larry's burned-out sixties accent.

LARRY: This is Dad's burned-out twenties accent.

MARK: This is Dad's burned-out-all-the-time accent.

LARRY: Shh, let's, let's not be too cruel, here. Okay, well, that was one supposedly unbiased view of Europe. Dan, do you want to say one that is, that contains no obscenities?

DANNY: *(sarcastically)* Bleeeeeep. *(something indecipherable)* . . . from a train.

LARRY: What was from a train? Oh, wait, wait, here we go, Dan met this gorgeous movie starlet from California on a train, and he . . . he got her phone number and they write to each other and they get presents for each other and he's gonna go to California and go out with her!

(Alas, if only this actually happened. What Danny is referring to is when Mark got food poisoning on the trip, suffered horrible diarrhea, and had to fling his underpants out the window of a moving train onto the beautiful Portuguese countryside.)

MARK: *(whispers to Danny)*

DANNY: *(cracking up)* What's that, Mark? No, I didn't get into her pants! How dare you?

LARRY: Oh, we can't say that on Festivus.

(A recording of German accordion music begins to play in the background.)

DAD: *(a mixture of German and English)* Was sie sagen ist ganz unrichtig. Wann wir in Europa zusammen waren, ich war der konig. Und die family war una gute familie. Nur in Verenienten Staten ist es nicht die selbe. Sie sind stark, sie sind verrukt, sie sind alter, aber ich bin der konig *dieses family, verstehen sie?* Vee are not in Europe! *And venn wir zuruck zum Europe gehen—*

(Translation: What they say is totally untrue. When we were together in Europe, I was the king. And the family was a good family. Only in the United States is it not the same. They're strong, they're crazy, they're older, but I am the king of this family, so you understand? We are not in Europe! And when we go back to Europe—)

LARRY: Okay, calm down, calm down.

DAD: *—denn bin ich wieder der konig!*

LARRY: Calm down.

DAD: *(doing a comically confused old man)* What? What? What?

(The tape is stopped and restarted.)

DAD: *(painfully slowly, in bad Russian) Kogda . . . delatsia . . . shto . . . belo . . . interesno . . .*

(This does not make any sense in either language.)

DANNY: What's "*delatsia?*"

DAD: Larry, *tovarish.*

LARRY: Yah.

DAD: *Govoreetsia shto—*

DANNY: What language is that?

DAD: Shto . . . Soon-Yi . . .

(It really sounds like "soon yi.")

DAD: *Delalee fmestye feh savyetskeeyeh Sayoozh!*

(This seems to mean, "Larry, comrade, talk that the sons did together to the Soviet Union!"

Translated from Dad to English, it means, "Larry, talk about how you and Danny went to Russia with your class.")

LARRY: What Dad is trying to say here is that in Februrary nineteen eighty-five, Dan and me and the rest of the Russian class went over to Russia.

DAD: Dan-*ny*.

LARRY: What?

THE FORD FESTIVA

KELLY BLUE BOOK RETAIL: $1,750–$2,150
EPA FUEL ECONOMY: City: 35 Highway: 42
AVAILABLE ENGINES: 63-hp, 1.3-liter I-4
AVAILABLE TRANSMISSIONS: 3-speed automatic, 5-speed manual w/OD
Specs listed are for 1993 model

This affordable subcompact replaced the Fiesta and in turn was produced until 1994, when it in turn was supplanted by the Aspire. It got unbelievable gas mileage, but it's even more amazing how much stuff you can cram in the back of one of these little cars. The hatchback is simple to operate and can be used even by the most nearsighted and uncoordinated of people. It's also very dependable. One slight drawback is the automatic seat belts: as soon as you start the car they almost leap for your throat. It's a little disturbing. The ride is smooth up to about seventy mph; after that it begins to rattle a bit. All in all, the 1993 Ford Festiva is pleasant, dependable transportation for a reasonable price. The authors of The Real Festivus are proud to recommend it. Three and a half stars.

The Festiva bears no relation whatsoever to the Festivus holiday, but the two words are similar.

DAD: Dan-*ny*.

LARRY: Dan-*ny* and Lar-*ry* and the Russian class went over to Russia during a time when Konstantin Chernenko was sort of alive.

LARRY: And it was a lot of fun, and here, here, here we have an unbiased opinion on that from Mr. Dan O'Keefe, commonly known as—

(Whatever obscene name Larry has called Danny here is lost, as the next few seconds have been erased. The tape is stopped and restarted.)

LARRY: Well, what, what did we do?

DANNY: *(sounding depressed)* We, um, went on a plane. And the plane kind of went to Moscow. And we got out in Moscow, and we were in Moscow for a while. And we went to Vladimir and Suzdahl after that, and we came back to Moscow, and then we went to Leningrad, and went to Finland, and then we came back. And while we were—

LARRY: Alright, Dan, Dan! Tell me, Dan, what was the temperature in Moscow?

DANNY: Gee, I don't know.

LARRY: *(as if to a retarded child)* I think it was twenty degrees below, wasn't it, Dan?

DANNY: Yep.

LARRY: Well, we, we had some good times there.

DANNY: *(monotone)* Oh yeah.

LARRY: I don't want to mention the twenty-three East

Germans in my bedroom, but what did *you* do, Dan?

DANNY: What did I do, uh . . . well, let me see; it was a while ago. Well, we went sightseeing on that, that, that . . .

LARRY: *(contemptuously)* Bus?

DANNY: Intourist. *(the Soviet tourist agency)*, bus, yeah, that's what it was. Intourist. And we saw incredible amounts of cathedrals—

LARRY: Too many.

DANNY: —and churches, too many churches, yeah.

LARRY: The Russians have this, have this, ah—

DANNY: Thing about cathedrals.

LARRY: Yeah.

DANNY: They have these—

LARRY: They hate religion, supposedly, but—

DANNY: —these pictures of, like, guys with these nails through their hands.

LARRY: *(you idiot)* Yeah . . . well, that was Jesus.

DANNY: Yeah, I guess so.

MOM: Did you meet any people?

LARRY: *(covering)* We, we, well, ah, yeah—

DANNY: Larry, tell about this Austrian . . . Austrian . . . Austrian person.

LARRY: Aw, shut up, Dan. Denise was nothing.

DANNY: *(chuckling)* Oh, really?

LARRY: Shut up! Okay, well, I gotta tell about Denise. Mike Barr first met her, then I got her. Okay, let's go on—

(In second grade I vomited on Mike Barr's desk. Just thought I'd mention that.)

DANNY: *(giggles)*

LARRY: Okay. Well, it's . . . it's not funny, Dan.

DANNY: Denise was very funny.

LARRY: It was . . . it was . . . no. It's not.

DANNY: Larry, Larry, I heard it was very funny.

LARRY: Okay, then we went to this place called Vladimir and *(Russian pronunciation)* "Soooooozdahl." See, we had a, we had a tourist guide.

MARK: Are you done yet?

LARRY: We had a tourist guide who always called it "Sooooozdahl." And she kept wanting us to—

DANNY: *(quoting the guide)* "Copper shits!"

LARRY: Yes.

DANNY: "There's copper shits on this cathidrill!"

(The guide was talking about copper sheets used as roofing.)

LARRY: Yes, she was, took around to see all these "chorchess"—

(Meaning churches.)

DANNY: "Tartar-Mongol yoke!"

LARRY: Yeah, well, I'll tell you about that. Okay, ah, these "chorchess" always had, had these "copper shits" on the "cross-piss."

(Crosspiece.)

MARK: *(laughs)*

LARRY: And we, we never quite understood what that meant. And they, these Russians are always talking about this thing called the "Tartar-Mongol yoke."

(This refers to when the Asiatic peoples called the Tartars and Mongols ruled what is now Russia.)

DAD: What are, what are "copper shits?"

LARRY: "Copper shits" were, were on top of the "cross-piss."

DANNY: It's what happens when you eat pennies. *(belches)*

(Danny had obviously been saving that one up for a long time.)

LARRY: No, Dan, that's not funny.

MOM: *(Russian accent)* Zey are shits uff kupper!

DAD: Shits of copper? Oh, you mean sheets! Sheets!

LARRY: *(sarcastically)* Very good, Dad!

DAD: *(Russian accent)* Now I understand!

LARRY: Okay. Well, then we went back to—oh God, I broke the . . I broke a . . . I broke a bed in Moscow. I'll tell you about that some other time. Okay.

(Larry clearly wants to be asked about this incident.)

DANNY: He broke it with, by jumping on it with, with fourteen fully clothed East Germans; don't let him mislead you.

MARK: They were all male!

DAD: *(concerned)* But they were fully clothed?

DANNY: Yeah, they were.

LARRY: Yes, Dad. We went to Leningrad after that, which is a cool place, and there was a—

DANNY: M-members of the, of the Women's Mustache Growing Team from East Germany.

LARRY: That's not funny, Dan. That is not funny at all. Dan, the women all shave enough, okay?

DANNY: No, they don't.

(Danny and Larry chuckle)

DAD: *(Irish accent)* Larry, is it true what you told me, that all the girls are three feet high in . . . in the northern parts of Russia?

LARRY: Well, they are pretty masculine—

DANNY: Those aren't girls, Dad, those are . . . those are . . . those are coyotes.

(See the photo at left—we're being awfully hard on Russian women for kids who looked like this.)

Uh oh! Lock up the women!

LARRY: Sled dogs.

DAD: *(uproarious laughter)*

LARRY: No, but, um, no. They, no, the women are pretty masculine, they'll beat on you—

DAD: Is it true that under the Soviet Union system of socialism—

LARRY: Alright, alright.

DAD: —sled dogs are being given an education?

DANNY: What?

LARRY: Well, they will kill you if you so much as *look* at their sled dogs.

(Larry is referring to a cartoon by Sam Gross published in National Lampoon *magazine in the mid-eighties. It shows a dingy Laundromat. A young guy is doing his laundry next to a dirty, hairy, older couple. The old, hairy guy is leaning over, saying: "You have only to look at my wife's intimate undergarments, and I shall be forced to kill you.")*

DANNY: *(disbelieving)* Sled dogs are being given an education?

LARRY: Okay, well, we, we had a fun time in Leningrad and we, we—

DANNY: Oh, and we went walking on the Baltic *(Sea, frozen over at the time)*. That was—

LARRY: I didn't do that, 'cause I was afraid I was gonna fall in.

DANNY: I didn't do it either, actually.

LARRY: Well, let's just assume we did.

DAD: Dan's not so good for walking on water.

(Silence.)

LARRY: Yes, indeed. Okay, um.

(Danny and Larry chuckle.)

DAD: Okay, now we're going to ask Mom for the annual summary of what has happened in the family. Now, remember that the last Festivus was around Fourth of July weekend in nineteen eighty-four; we've gone almost a year and a half since then. Debby, come tell us what has happened.

MOM: *(deep breath)* Okay. It's hard to summarize this . . . long period, wherein lots of different things have been happening. We've been playing recently some Billy Joel songs, and—I like the, I like one that's called "Moving Out." And I don't mean it in the same cynical way, but I think—

LARRY: Dan does.

MOM: —the boys are starting be moving out, ah, sometimes we seem to be heading in different directions; they're going off on trips on their own. Sometimes we come to Vermont with two or even one or even zero kids, but this Thanksgiving we're all together, and I hope and believe we'll have other times when we are, even though people are going in different directions. Ah, I see that sort of thing, ah, happening with the Balls . . .

(The Balls are our first cousins; the children of my

mother's sister. Their name has been and continues to be a source of great hilarity.)

MOM: . . . where all the kids are in different places, especially Richard, who's off working for CARE in Africa, Larry Ball has actually gotten married—

LARRY: *(really into it, for some reason)* Yeah!

MOM: —with a great family occasion that we all went to, and Danny was in Larry's wedding, reading very eloquently from the Bible.

DAN: Larry tried to get me to sit down, but I wouldn't.

LARRY: No, no, no, no.

(At our cousin Larry Ball's wedding, Larry O'Keefe was heckling Danny silently with obscene hand gestures, as he read from the Song of Solomon.*)*

MOM: It was a great occasion, and there'll be more occasions of all kinds, some of which we can't even begin to predict. Danny will be moving out, but coming back also. He has put in an early application to Harvard, and we don't know exactly what will come of it, but we're convinced that he will end up either there or some other terrific place. I'm moving out of Manhattanville *(College)*, with mixed feelings, it's too much work for too little money. Dan *(our father)* at work isn't absolutely sure where everything is going; he has been made an Issue Editor (*of the* Reader's Digest) recently, and many things seem to be up in the air but have great potential. The boys are doing interesting things in and out of school; they seem to be having an interesting, exciting, and mysterious social life—*(she giggles)*

LARRY: Mom, you can understand why we don't—

MOM: Interesting things at, in their academic lives, and extracurricular things, and I think they're gonna say some, give some information about some of that, though *(dripping with irony)* I would hope not about everything.

DAD: There were quite a few plays in the last year and a half. And Mark appeared in *The Boyfriend* in the Bell *(Middle)* School play—

LARRY: *(garbled insult directed at Mark, probably to the effect that he played the part of the "Girlfriend.")*

DAD: —playing the Boyfriend, and he sang this song.

(Dad now sings a stirring rendition of part of the song "I Could Be Happy with You, Dear, if You Could Be Happy with Me" from that musical.)

DANNY: *(laughing)* Oh, God.

LARRY: *(pretending to be fair.)* Let's hear him out.

DAD: . . . and so on, and he also sang, well, he won't sing it for us tonight. But he also sang . . .

(He now sings part of the song "Just a Room.")

DAD: . . . and we have a tape of it somewhere. But he won't sing it. Now, Danny and Larry—

LARRY: *(apparently excited at the sound of his name)* Yeah!

DAD: —were in three plays.

MARK: *(hurt)* I haven't spoken yet, Dad!

DAD: Now boys, will you do something from *Pippin*?

DANNY, LARRY, and MARK: No.

DAD: Are you willing to sing, *(singing)* "Think about your life, Pippin!"

LARRY: Let's, let's not.

DAD: *(still singing)* "Think about your life . . ."

LARRY: Okay . . .

DAD: *(making up lyrics now)* Because it's full of strife, Pippin! *(somberly, obviously not talking about Pippin anymore)* It's full of strife, yes.

(The tape is stopped and restarted.)

DAD: Both of them, both boys, were in three major high school plays! They were both onstage as stars in *Pippin*—

LARRY: Not at the same time.

DAD: —both onstage as stars of *Scapino*, continuously—

DANNY: We weren't stars in either one!

DAD: —and they were in *Museum*! And Larry now has something from *Museum*, here's Larry.

LARRY: *(back to his damn stoner voice)* Well, *Museum* was a major breakthrough, since it starred two O'Keefes in the two starring roles, and now we're gonna do a little scene from it. My name is Michael Wall—

DANNY: I . . . I was the lead.

LARRY: Yeah, okay. He, Dan, was the *(contemptuously)* Guard at a museum, and I'm a, I'm a photographer who's set up all his equipment, and the guard is, is really getting me mad. Okay, ready? Okay.

(silence.)

DANNY: Larry's just setting up his equipment now. You can't hear it, but he's just like, setting it up.

LARRY: That's not funny, Dan.

DANNY: It is funny.

LARRY: Shh.

(Danny and Larry now do a scene from their high school production of Tina Howe's play Museum. *The scene involves a smarmy photographer trying to get an annoyingly talkative museum guard to let him photograph the artworks, even though it's against museum regulations.)*

DANNY: *(depressed)* Ta da.

LARRY: *(pleased)* Alright, that's pretty good. Okay, ah, that was *Museum*, performed by—

DANNY: *(suicidal)* Ah, it sucked.

LARRY: Yeah, okay. Performed by Dan and Larry O'Keefe in the two main roles. And now we have the ever-popular, perpetual freshman; you know him, you love him, you can't live without him; it's Mark O'Keefe! *(imitates the roar of a crowd)*

DANNY: Mark O'Keefe? Oh, my God! Can I touch you?

(Mark giggles.)

LARRY: Shh. Shh. Cut that out.

DANNY: Can I be your friend?

MARK: *(laughing)* Hands off the merchandise!

LARRY: Okay. Mr. Mark O'Keefe.

MARK: Yeah.

LARRY: I understand you've been, you've been doing some work along the lines of cross-country—

DANNY: *(loud stage whisper)* Dweeeeeeeeeeeb!

LARRY: —running.

MARK: *(laughing)* Fuck you!

LARRY: Okay.

MARK: Yes, that is true. I mean the rumors are true.

LARRY: Ah, well, okay. Um, what, what exactly constitutes this—

MARK: I'm a, I'm a—

LARRY: Shh! Shh! What exactly constitutes this cross-country running?

MARK: Well, uh, basically you just run. For miles.

(Danny, Larry, and Mark giggle.)

LARRY: Hey, that's real good. That's brilliant.

MARK: I mean, I mean, but that's not it. I mean sometimes you collapse.

LARRY: Well, is this a matter for competition, or for endurance more?

MARK: Well . . . ah . . . I did it in races.

LARRY: Okay, um. Well that, that's pretty good. What is, what are your records, basically? Are you—

MARK: Well, in the mile point eight, I got a . . . um . . . like twelve minutes and like fifty-two seconds.

LARRY: Is . . . is that spectacular? For your age group?

MARK: Yeah, it is.

LARRY: Well, that's good. That's really good.

MARK: And this is on . . . this is on a cross-country course.

LARRY: Okay, um, what other things have you done at Horace Greeley *(high school)* in your first, and may I add, freshman year?

DAN: *(says something indecipherable about Mark)*

LARRY: Shh, Dan, that's not nice. Let's go.

MARK: I've just been my magnetic self.

DANNY: *(scoffing)* Drugs.

LARRY: —senior girls have just gone "Aaaaaaaaaaaah!" and have just thrown their arms around you.

MARK: Oh, please.

LARRY: Oh, no, you should be flattered.

DANNY: They're always like pounding on your arms and stuff.

(They were not. But Danny's first girlfriend used to playfully punch him in the arms, really hard, and we guess he wanted to believe everyone was going through the same thing.)

LARRY: What?

DANNY: You have to carry "Senior-Off."

(Presumably, this is an imaginary product that you spray on yourself to keep high school senior girls away.)

DANNY: *(proudly) That's* a funny joke.

LARRY: Shh, shh.

MARK: I thought it was quite funny, myself.

(In fact, it is not.)

DANNY: Tell us something about yourself.

LARRY: Yeah, what do you like about *(Horace)* Greeley *(High School)*.

MARK: It's . . . *(searching)* . . . good. *(chuckles like a moron)* Well, there's a lot more freedom, and there's a lot more grades.

DANNY: *(amazed at the stupidity of the answer)* A lot more *grades?*

MARK: No, I mean grades as in *people* grades. You know, like ninth and tenth. You know.

(Silence. Mark chuckles nervously.)

LARRY: Uh, anything else? Alright, one last thing, all of us are at the moment trying out for the Greeley musical, which is called *Is There Life After High*

School? As of now we have all been basically called back. And, which means we all might get a part in the show, and we're looking forward to that. Alright.

DANNY: My guess is we will get in because they'll think it would be cute to have three brothers on the same stage.

(Actually, we all did get in, but were not cute.)

(The tape is stopped and restarted, and we hear the piano chords of "New York State of Mind" *once again.)*

DAD: So where do we stand? What's the score? What's the theme? I guess the theme is, "Life Goes On." Life goes on. Granny has gone. On. The last transition. Danny, before we have another Festivus, will go to college, and may not be here for the next Festivus. And indeed, since we've only been having Festivi a year and a half apart, the next one could be just before Larry . . . goes. I could be retired. Life goes on.

WHAT WE'VE LEARNED FROM THIS ONE

THAT FESTIVUS CONSISTS of more than we remembered of remembering those who have left the rest of us forever. That teenagers are unbearably dumb and annoying, even when they're you. And finally, it may not be "cool" to say so, but this tape reveals above all that Billy Joel continues to totally and thoroughly rock the tri-state area.

WHAT YOU WILL NEED FOR YOUR AUTHENTIC FESTIVUS

Now, if after reading all that, you're still set on celebrating this thing as we used to, you will need the following things:

Some Type of Family Unit

Outlying relatives like grandparents and cousins can be included, that's authentic: we had a guest at one Festivus, our lovely and intelligent cousin Julie, who appears on the 1984 tape. Now she lives in Hong Kong. This is probably unrelated to what she saw that night.

A Turkey or Other Dead Animal to Eat

This is not a holiday for vegetarians. A true Festivus meal has to include something that felt pain as it died. Sorry, hippie.

Champagne

Can be cheap crap, as long as it's fizzy. "Bourbon Champagne" is acceptable, but if you substitute it you will also need a:

Puke Bucket

Play-Doh

Do they still make that stuff? We hope so. Don't worry about your kids; we ate tons of it, and we're okay. Mostly.

Stupid Homemade Hats

For material, paper or tinfoil is recommended. Dry-cleaning bags are not recommended, as you will die.

Mournful Irish Death Music

Alternately, some mournful music related to your particular ethnicity. As long as it's not peppy. Ideally it will deal with fighting the British, and since numerous peoples suffered under the British Empire, there's a lot to choose from.

Willie Nelson's "Stardust" and *Billy Joel's Greatest Hits*

Preferably on LP records, but most people don't have turntables these days. LPs were better than CDs. I remember when ice cream was a nickel.

Clock and Bag

A simple alarm clock and a brown paper grocery bag will do.

Sign Indicating Opposition to Fascism

It doesn't have to be obscene. But YAY, FASCISM! or LET'S GO, FASCISM! signs are just not acceptable.

Tape Recorder and Tapes

When recording your memories of the year, you want

that nice pop, crackle, and hiss to be mixed in with your recriminations and laughter. "Burning" a "CD" is too modern, and "illuminating" a "vellum parchment" is too old-fashioned and will take too long.

CONCLUSION

Listening to these tapes has been as odd an experience for me as reading the transcripts must be for you. I haven't really thought about this holiday in any detail in years. And it now seems that, far from the entertainingly bitter Festivus portrayed on television, the real Festivus was, in retrospect, heartwarmingly peculiar and occasionally, peculiarly heartwarming.

We may not have thought so at the time, but we were lucky to have Festivus. It was a celebration of family, and an exorcism of the demons that menaced it. In the Gertrude Stein opera *In Circles*, which we heard a lot of on this holiday, the title song concludes:

I leave you there
Do not, do not despair
Remain in a circle
And do not despair.

That's the basic idea. Remain in a circle and do not despair. And buy other copies of this book for your friends. It makes a lovely gift.

Dan O'Keefe has been a night security guard, a camp counselor, a supermarket cashier, and more recently a writer and producer for such TV shows as *Seinfeld*, *Drew Carey*, *The Tonight Show with Jay Leno*, *Married...with Children*, and *Listen Up*. He has also written for magazines such as the *Harvard Lampoon*, the *National Lampoon*, *Cracked Magazine*, and once even *Seventeen*, where everyone smelled really good, even the dudes. In the event of a disfiguring fire, his remains can be identified by a chipped lower left molar and two broken toes on his right foot. He was born in New York, lives in Los Angeles, and will die on the disputed Kurile island chain between Russia and Japan.